Gehrmann et al. (Eds.)
Social Work and Social Work Studies

Social Work and Social Work Studies

Cooperation in Europe 2000

Documentation from International Colloquium
Frankfurt am Main 1993

Edited by
Gerd Gehrmann, Klaus D. Müller and
Robert Ploem

Deutscher Studien Verlag · Weinheim 1994

About the Editors:

Prof. Dr. Gerd Gehrmann, Dipl.-Päd., 1942, teaches at the Fachhochschule Frankfurt.

Prof. Dr. Klaus D. Müller, Dipl.-Päd., 1944, teaches at the Fachhochschule Frankfurt.

Drs. Robert Ploem, 1950, teaches at the Hogeschool van Amsterdam.

Die Deutsche Bibliothek – CIP-Einheitsaufnahme

Social work and social work studies : cooperation in Europe 2000 ; documentation from international colloquium Frankfurt am Main 1993 / ed. by Gerd Gehrmann ... – Weinheim : Deutscher Studien Verlag, 1994
ISBN 3-89271-506-8
NE: Gehrmann, Gerd [Hrsg.]

Printed by: Druck Partner Rübelmann, 69502 Hemsbach
Serial cover design: Atelier Warminski, 63654 Büdingen
Printed in Germany

ISBN 3 89271 506 8

Inhalt:

Einleitung:

Die Entwicklung zu einem vereinten Europa schreitet - wenn auch nicht immer kontinuierlich - voran. Diese Entwicklung hat eine sich ständig verdichtende Zusammenarbeit zwischen europäischen Hochschulen zur Folge.

Die in diesem Band dargestellten überarbeiteten Beiträge des 3. Internationalen Colloquiums über innovative Entwicklungen in Praxis, Lehre und Forschung in der Sozialen Arbeit in Frankfurt am Main (April 1993) zeugen von einer besonderen Qualität der europäischen Zusammenarbeit. Es sind ausschließlich Ergebnisse und Erkenntnisse aus bi- oder tri-nationalen Projekten einer intensiven inhaltlichen Zusammenarbeit der beteiligten Hochschulen.

Diese Hochschul-Kooperation hat bereits eine mehrjährige Geschichte und entstammt ursprünglich den Hochschulkontakten der Hogeschool van Amsterdam, der heutigen Manchester Metropolitan University und deutschen Fachhoschschulen, die sich 1989 zum ersten Mal in Amsterdam trafen, um eine Standortbestimmung und Problemauflistung zur Sozialen Arbeit in Lehre, Praxis und Forschung vorzunehmen.

Das 2. Internationale Colloquium fand 1991 in Manchester statt. Da weitgehend der gleiche Personenkreis daran teilnahm, konnte die Arbeit die Ergebnisse des ersten Workshops weiterführen. Das 3. Internationale Colloquium, dessen Beiträge wir hiermit veröffentlichen, war in der Kontinuität der Tagungen das bislang anspruchvollste. Dies konnte gelingen, weil aufgrund der inzwischen vierjährigen Zusammenarbeit gemeinsame Projekte mit berichtenswerten Ergebnissen stattgefunden haben und weil wir als Organisatoren auch deshalb eine stärkere Systematisierung und eine höhere Qualität der Beiträge erreichen konnten.

Die hier aufgenommenen überarbeiteten Referate in englischer Sprache sind auch unabhängig von der konkreten Tagung ein wichtiger Beitrag zur Thematik europäischer Zusammenarbeit und nationaler Entwicklungen unter einer vergleichenden Fragestellung.

Gerd Gehrmann / Klaus D. Müller / R. Ploem

1. Sozialarbeitsforschung und Methodenentwicklung in europäischer Dimension:

The Domaine of Social Work - Perspectives For the Profession - introductive statements -

Klaus D. Müller / Gerd Gehrmann

Social Work in Europe 2000 is developing in many different national streams and particularities, in spite of common origins and . common reasons for existance. This matter seems surprising, because of the manifold mutual personal and theoretical international links, especially between England, America, the Netherlands and Germany.

On the other hand we are facing different national traditions in our ways of thinking, our social welfare systems and laws. Andrew Cooper and John Pitts in their paper on "The Relationship between Trans-National European Social Work Research and Social Work Education" are stressing that these different ways of thinking in the different European countries are forming fairly high obstacles for joint ventures. These difficulties in understanding are shown in their research cooperation with French colleages. Their contribution to our colloquium is providing some ideas about what has to be considered in transnational research and exchange projects. They also give some hints how misunderstandings in European cooperation could arise.

Malcolm Payne adds the argument to take notice of ideological barriers in the British perspective on Europe deriving from its imperial history.

In trans-national research-projects we shall have to find a common. language or else we would remain in a partly fictious communication. In an ironical version: mock communication, mock understanding and mock agreements, like sometimes in absurd theatre or the political scenery.

These opinions were not directly opposed to by other contributions to the colloquium, but we could trace some hints in the-articles of Marc McLean, of Kate Brown and Mait Widmark/Ola Eriksson that we have got means for overcoming these national differences in understanding. With Mark Mclean we would suggest that qualitative research in the field of the patterns-of-meanings-analysis in research and in the training of future social workers could reach deep enough to trace a common basis on a European cultural background. We call this "Deutung" and hermeneutic understanding (Oevermann et al. 1979). We used the methodof the. "narrative interview"' which had been published in Germany by (Schtitze 1983 and Stidmersen'1983) for doing research on the everyday-practice of social workers in a design of learning by doing research with students of social work (Gehrmann /Müller 1992). The practice research was done with a concept of action research the importance of which Hans Oostrik is stressing for the development of methodology in social work.

The participating students and practitioners were able to gain insights in profes-

sional action and its individual and common interpretations and discrepancies.
These steps for a deeper understanding and assessement, which is a major concern of Geert van der Laan (see his aticle) could build a bridge of apprehension not only in transnational cooperation, but also in the cooperation between teachers of social work and students as well as between research workers and practitioners on a national level. Misunderstandings in the latter fields can be almost as deep as between members of different nations. The European nations have become multicultural and multi-ethnic societies. Multilateral understanding has become of vital importance for a survival of the democracies of many nations not only in the European Union (see v.Vliet, Hayes and Ranson).
Social work besides many other functions has always had that of an early alarm-system for societal crises. The professional tools and instruments for the analysis and assessment of social work therefore have to be developed more effectively, they have to become more sofisticated and handy at the same time, which seems to be contradictive but is not necessarily so.
We are convinced that.there is a good perspective in comparative projects in the education of social workers, when it comes to create a basis of transnational understanding. Kate Brown offers a very promising approach by introducing the comparative perspective. into the social work education without making groups of students and teachers travel abroad. This might to be an effective low-cost alternative to the intensive trinational workshops (Widmark/Eriksson), which have been regarded as very successful in many was. Our further cooperation and a comparative evaluation will have to be done to find out the pros. and cons of both models. We might perhaps discover that both models are serving different good purposes.
We have already pointed out that our primery concern is not that of transnational understanding in general but that of creating a vital. common base for the cooperation between our own colleges and among the different national members of our profession, the one we are qualifiing students for.
How can me minimize these difficulties inunderstanding?
We do not trust in very abstract theoretical levels of discourses, as many of our German colleagues are practicing in their intellectual "ivory towers", where this problem cannot be tackled efficiently. Our efforts to minimize misunderstandings in cooperation between partners who command of different languages and different theoretical backgrounds are focused on a direct interactive confrontation of researchers and practitioners.
The type of problems seems very simular. Like between transnational cooperants in Research and Education in Social Work, there is a different language between-research workers and social workers on the national level. In spite of the same background of values and institutional development we are facing quite a big communicative lag between academical disciplines and social work practice, sometimes even between social work practitioners. in different fields and research and teaching at schools of social work. The latter problem is that of a profession which has been driven into specialisation and diversification. At the same time it has

grown to a trade with a numerous number of actors on various levels. Its monstrosity and its multi-shaped-body'reveals its weekness in its brain. It is open for any influences and all kind of diversing interests.

Colleagues of neighbouring disciplines like sociology, psychology und educational science e.g. are still trying to define the problems in social work. At least in Germany we realize a gap between social work practice and theory, which very often had been developed from the disciplinary focuses of strangers to the profession. This gap between theory and prctice, of cause, does not only derive from the "colonalism" of the established academic professions; it seems to be a home-made product of the profession as well (we shall come to that.argument later). We know that theory always has the task to criticize and to comment on practice. Without the vital tention between theory and practice innovarive developments would be rare. Critique on the practice of social work is usefull. It could be of innovarive value, if it would be enriched by insider knowledge and the unevitable professional focus, and it should give assistance to the practitioner. Whenever these conditions are missing, critique though vital for the institutions and social work practice will be seen as destructive and not meeting the real conditions and therefore be effectless. Whenever we get too much of this kind of sometimes arrogant criticism the resistance among the practitioners will prevent any kind of progress.

The same problem arises when the language of researchers is too abstract and the methodology not meeting the needs of the profession of social work.

How can we overcome the difficulties of understanding between the social worker in practice and the research worker or the teachers of social work at the colleges? In the first place we shall.have to take to a communicative type of social science and research, appropriate for the development and evaluation of innovations in social work. Rather than the science type of research we will have to take to action research (see the article of Hans Oostrik) and communicative validation in a multimethod design. With many of our Dutch colleagues we believe in a strategy of reflected pragmatism as more adequate for the development of innovarive systems in practice and theory.

Reflected pragmatism in Germany seems to be a major offence against academic traditions, where social and other phenomena tend to be deeply examined ad inifinitum, searching for historical and philosophical implimentations and historical roots. (looking for historical roots is necessary I admit, but it should not prevent the occupation with practical innovations in the present situation).

This strategy tends to lead to a level of discourse which for the social worker is remaining a strange and hostile world. Unexplained and inadequate theory evoces a defensive attitude against theory.

What happens: research workers are claiming the (abstract) rights of the client, they give out warnings against a remote specialized social work in opposition to the client's lifestile, they critize social work asuming therapeutic methods and the metaphor of social illness. Social workers without theoretical and practical assistance take all the same to methods developed by psychiatry and psychology, be-

cause they seem so well structured and clear, *rendering* a scientific image. At the same time our profession very often is not able of telling cooperating members of other professions or politicians or the public what social workers are really doing and achieving when doing their jobs. We are very often still missing genuine and practicable methods of work and the vital genuine professional language.
Some kind of situation of distress we sometimes notice when cooperating with social workers in the field of practice. Practitioners in general social services are claiming to be in a too stressing situation, because they have to take on too many clients in bad working conditions, which would not allow them to develope a professional way of tackling social problems. Many of them after several years of practice seem to be worn out.
In this situation joint ventures of researchers and practitioners will have to take place: joint ventures in developening methods, instruments for structuring practice situations, for taking records and the processes and for evaluation.
In our cooperation with social workers we have learned that innovations in social work are more likely to take place, when it can be proved to the practitioners that everyday practice can be improved with useful methods. In many cases it became quite evident that innovations in the practical methods showed the limitation of existing organizational frames. In these situations we had to do organisational development. This became important because exsiting organizational structures have not been develloped according in the line of agencies producing social services at all or to obsolet professional standards. Very often the management of a social service institution could be characterized as being "structurally delittante", which means that the processes of producing managers in social work organizations either do not favour the choice of qualified chefs or do not provide adequate schooling for the management of social organizations, see *Gehrmann/Müller 1993*.
Back to the level of practical innovations: social workers are open to accept the first steps of professional concelling. By helping them to find priorities it sometimes is posssible show a system of selfmanagent in their practice, organizing their cases one by one. This of course does not work without the agreement of the head managers.
Some of our efforts did not succeed at all, e.g. when the social workers could not be convinced of the usefullness and help we could offer or when the head management did not agree.
In the above mentioned dilemma of all kind of difficulties in the communication between research workers in social work and social workers in practice a common language meanings and last not least theory of action has to be found. A theoretically minded practical means of communication between theory (Research practice). Where shall we look for it? How will it have to look like? Which *criteria* to meet? More questions than answers are available. And it is one of our habits to produce more and more questions. We are trained in producing more intelligent questions than answers valid for at least the future in order to favour active solutions. Practitioners are looking for answers more than for questions. It is our task to ask

them for some patiance but not for a too long time, sooner or later we have to offer some pratical support.
Social workers, teaching at the Columbia University, supported by the National Association of Social Workers, have claimed that the domination of social work by other disciplines and their methods should come to an end. With their concept "PIE" (Person in Environment) they introduced a new language for social work, a language and method for analysing social problems seen through the eyes of socialworkers and not through those of other professions *(Karls/Wandrei* 1992)
Their annoyance developed when they realized that the mainstream *further* professional training provided the DSM III R to social workers, an advanced anamnetic instrument of the psychiatry. The annoyed social workers .tested the PIE in experimental situations (control-group with DSM). If you take a closer look on it you will find out that it is a very useful instrument focusing on social role and social environment in the first place and not an psychical deficiencies like the DSM.
This instrument for analyzing social problems is already been practiced in the social work education in Amsterdam, Karl-Ernst Hesser and Anjo van Hour have told us about their experiences with the PIE. It has turned out to be a handy and genuin instrument of social work in any assessment phase (like in the case managment (Lowy 1988, Wendt 1991, Ballew/Mink 1991). At the same time it has a major significance for the communication among social workers and between social workers and research workers.
At the same time it can be used for the research on the local, national and international distinction of the qualitiy and spreading of social problems. Sorry, that I cannot go into detail.
The most important issue in this approach is the way of thinking, its focus on the lifesituation of clients, which can easily combined with the concept of the "Neue Fachlichkeit". This concept - New Professionalism - has already been developed in 1977.
It is claiming that the social worker should not act anymore as a highly specialized expert in "treating" individualized deficiencies of the client, he / she having a problem, which he/she would have to solve on his own. The social worker's "treatment" used to be a kind of verbal councelling or "therapy". This was critized, because even though not putting the burden of personal guilt apon her/his shoulders, the client still was individually "treated" in a setting of councelling: meaning vertually that in traditional case work he/she was treated as patient/ client who would then set out to cope with his/her "problems".
The "Neue Fachlichkeit" conceptualized the situation of the client in a different way, such' as follows.' The client of social work is confronted with social problems which are of societal origin. She/he is part 'of them and has some definable personalparts in it. This takes-into consideration that not every person in the same social situation will become a client of social work and that she/he has to develop own efforts to get out of it. Selfactivation therefore is a major goal of social work.
Social work agencies were seen as services to those who cannot cope with their sit-

uations, they were seen as organizations ready for reform, inovative development. Social services were seen as service institutions for the sake of citizens; a recent development is stressing this innovarive tendency; empowerment and user-involvement in social services (see *Croft/Beresford).*
The concept of the "Neue Fachlichkeit" was developed among academics, dicussed and appreciated allover, be it hardly left traces in *the* social work practice. To our opinion a major reason was that apart from its language, it mainly offered new imperatives and demands to the practitioners which they could not meet. They had to work in structures which were not open to any method known, they very often did not know how to start innovation and they did not command of methods, which could meet the demands of this concept.
Since the middle of the eighties the profession has made a big step forward. The socio-ecological approach (The PIE. is just one smaller part of it) has given an enormous input both to theory- and practice-methods of social work. Theory conceptualized the client in'a problematic situation induced by societal influences and structures she/he cannot cope (Gehrmann/Müller 1990) without professional support. She/he has not acquired aequate skills and abilities to cope the challanges (Hesser 1991) which occur in her/his interacting with the socio-ecological surroundings. Do you notice the difference? We are saying: the client is faced with challenges derived as we explained and not: she/he has problems! In accordance with all codes of ethics for social workers we know(like that of the British Association of Social Workers (BASW 1990) the clients are conceptualized as "normal" persons faced with challenges and not as mentally, physically or socially ill. In our language we shall have to express this new way of thinking.
The profession of social work in this perspective has its focus on the interference of the individual with its social environment which as the micro-level is influenced by the meso- and macro structures of the society (Bronfenbrenner 1976). In the same way the individual is influencing its social environment by acting (Giddens 1990). The Domaine of social work: not the "treatment" of the individual on its own neither the social structures allone but the individual in its social environment, in its nische is the professional focus and phere of action. We have to know the circumstances in the individual *social* biography, which have lead to the problematic situation, to the challenge she/he cannot cope with. We shall have to find out which supporting and which endangering elements (material, institutional, personal) the nische consists of, which has also provided some place and strategies to survive so far and on the existing improvable level. Where are the traps? We have to get to know about the hopes, perspectives and strenghts of the client and the social network which could be activated (see Environment Activation-Method-Gehrmann/ Müller 1993) and were a support plan could get a grip.
Not only in America we can trace the new discussion on genuin social work theory and methods. In Germany the development on the socio-ecological concept started in the eighties. Colleagues of the Deutsche Gesellschaft fur Sozialarbeit like Albert Huhlure, Hubert Oppl and Wolf Reiner Wendt (1986) introduced this para-

digm into German social work in several publications. Klaus Müller and I joined a little later an started research and development in what the Americans (Karls and Wandrei) called the "domaine of social work".

We would like to show the significance of this new paradigm of social work by giving an exemple from our practice in research.

We defined the domaine of social work as the professional area where social problems are identified with a geniune focus of social workers (like in the PIE) in the overlapping sphere of the inividual and his/her social *surrounding* area and structures, the sociotope, the nische of the life-situtíon. The professional domaine of social work on the line of competencies are those taks' and qualifications in service for the clients which are predominently performed by social workers and not by *neighbouring* professions, like psychologists, medical doctors,-therapists and others.

Especially in institutions, where social workers have to cooperate with these neighbouring professions we found that the domaine Of social work can be traced in reality. Certain tasks and qualifications were not only claimed by social workers, they were all the same expected from the social workers by the *other* cooperating professions. In one institution of this kind *e.g.* a social-psychiatric center for the *early recognition* and treatment of handicaps of children the'social workers claimed for themselves - and they were expected to perform - special tasks:

- give advice and assistance to the clients and to the colleages (medical doctors, psychologists,therapists etc) in all matters concerning the social laws, family laws, social insurances, the hole system of social support,
- lead the negotiations and the communication with all kind of necessary institu-ions in the social network,
- councelling in everyday-life situation, offering support in all social and material ways,
- linking the clients with the supporting agencies by encouraging the self-help activities of the clients and giving a non protective support,
- visiting of the clients in their homes (if invited) and looking at their social surroundings and social networks.

Indeed, the social workers were the only, who were supposed to, were trained for and competent to do this work inside and outside the institution.

We are going to continue this kind of research and we are very confident to discover these an other tasks and qualifications, which are at first hand thejob of social workers. We also discovered some overlapping tasks and competences with those of psychologists and therapists, like councelling along the line of psychotherapy, but they did not occur very often and they always ment a competitive confrontation with the psychologists.

What is the meaning of this exemple for the international colloquium?

By doing research and developement about the domaine of social work we will be looking for stepstones towards an action theory for social work despite of all criticism from the established professions around. Some of them are not very much

ahead of social work. Educational science e.g. only lately became a real academic discipline, when it became a critical social sience (Thiersch 1986) with empirical research on its matters.
Whenever any other established discipline tries to describe a professional practice in everyday-life outside the university, it will be stuck in the same kind of difficulties as social work. Do we really need the one and only theory of social work in oder. to be recocnized as an academic discipline of its own? I do not think so. All the well established disciplines do not have one setting of theory and methodology. The key question of social work seems to be, whether social work is developing conceptions to define its social function, its practical tasks and its own focus on practice and its own methods for its performance in action.
Facing the latest developments towards the domaine of social work, its help the inanlyzing of social problems and its methodology, we are quite confident: Social work is on its way striving for disciplinary recognition. A lot of practice research will still have to be done.
Perhaps this colloquium will help to combine the discussions in a productive way in transnational coperation, to exchange experiences in research and the development of methods and to build up new cooperations and partnerships among the participating colleagues. From our own experience we know that international cooperation and the backing up by colleagues can help to support activities at home.

Literature

Ballew,R.J / Mink, G.: Was ist Case-Management? in: Wendt,W.R.: Unterstützung fallweise, Freiburg 1991.

Boulton, David: Doing Research Using Official Data, in this book.

Bronfenbrenner, Uri: Ökologische Sozialisationsforschung, Stuttgart 1976.

Brown, Kate: Framework for Understanding Comparative Social Welfare, in this book.

Cooper, Andrew/Pitts,J ohn: Ironic Investigations: The Relationship Between Transnational European Research and Social Work Education, in this book.

Croft, S./Berefaord, P.: User-Involvement in Social Services: Learning From Good Practice in Europe, in this book.

van Flier, Pieter: Development of Cooperation With Former Colonies, in this book.

Gehrmann, G./Müller K.D.: Professionalät in der Sozialarbeit, socialmanagement 1/1991.

Gehrmann, G./Müller K.D.: Forschendes Lernen als Strategie der Praxisreflexion, Weinheim 1992

Gehrmann, G./Müller, K.D.:Die Environment-Aktivierungs-Methode Sozialmagazin 4/1993

Gehrmann, G./Müller K.D.: Management in sozialen Organisationen Regensburg 1993.

Giddens, Anthony: Die Konstitution der Gesellschaft, Frankfurt/New York 1988.

Hayes, D./Ranson, J.: Immigration Control and Deportation - Implications for Social Work, in this book.

Hesser Karl-Ernst / van Hout, Anjo: Forschungsantrag zur Methodenentwicklung, Amsterdam 1992.

Earls E. J./ Wandrei, K.: PIE - A New Language for Social Work, New York 1992.

van der Laan, Geert: An Etiquette for Social Workers, in this book.

Lowy, Louis: Case Management in der Sozialarbeit, in Mühlfeld u.a.(Hrsg): Brennpunkte Sozialer Arbeit, Heft Soziale Einzelhilfe, Frankfurt 1988.

McLean, Marc: The Appropriateness of Appropriation, the Authority of knowledge, empowerment and inner reform: Some Aspects of qualitative Research, in this book.

Mühlum, A./ Olschowy, G./ Oppl, H./ Wendt, W.R.: Umwelt - Lebenswelt Frankfurt am Main 1986

Oevermann, U. / Allert, T. / Konau, E. / Krambeck, J.: Die Methodologie einer objektiven Hermeneutik und ihre allgemeine forschungslogische Bedeutung in den Sozialwissenschaften, in Soeffner u.a.(Hrsg): Interpretative Verfahren in den Sozial- und Text-Wissenschaften, Stuttgart 1979.

Oostrik, Hans: Action Research as Means of Methodology Development in Social Work,. in this book.

Payne, Malcolm: The Effect of British Policy and Idiological Imperatives on Promoting European Links in Social Work Education, in this book.

Stidmersen, Ilse: Hilfe, ich ersticke in Texten - eine Anleitung zur Aufarbeitung narrativer Interviews, Neue Praxis 3/1983.

Schütze, Fritz: Biographieforschung und narratives Interview, Neue Praxis 3,/1983

Thiersch, Hans: Die Erfahrung der Wirklichkeit, Weinheim und München 1986

Wendt, W.R.: Die Handhabung der sozialen Unterstützung, in Wendt (Hrsg): Unterstützung fallweise, Freiburg 1991.

Widmark-Nielssen, M./Eriksson,O.: Experiences From Three Intensive Courses, in this book.

1.1 About the importance of European cooperation in research and methodology development for social work.

Karl-Ernst H. Hesser

With this contribution I would like to make a plea for more co-operation in research and methodology development for social work and social work studies. I would like to do so by successively discussing the following issues:

I. Recent developments in practice and theory of social work in the nineties.
II. The start of the co-operation between the 'Fachhochschule Frankfurt, Abteilung Sozialpädagogik' and the 'Hogeschool van Amsterdam/Produktgroep Methodiekontwikkeling'.
III. The expansion of the co-operation with the 'Stockholm Universitet/Socialhögskolan' and the new plans.
IV. The implementation of the results of international co-operation in programmes, curricula for social work studies.

I. Recent developments in practice and theory of social work in the nineties.

For this part of my contribution I gratefully used an article by Peter van Lieshout, head of the Nederlands Instituut voor Zorg en Welzijn (N.I.Z.W. [Dutch Institute for Care and Welfare]), Published under the title 'Zorg en welzijn als antenne voor her functioneren van de samenleving' (care and welfare as an antenna for the functioning of society), in 'Social Sector', June/July 1991, as well as the lecture of 1992 by Harry Wouters, project leader of the Produktgroep Methodiekontwikkeling at the Hogeschool van Amsterdam, entitled 'Scanning the future'. In doing so I would like to give an outline of trends and developments of practiceand theory of social work from a Dutch point of view. I seem to observe these developments taking place in other countries as well. This will come out in the discussion.

a. A number of cracks in our reality is noted:
   1. The welfare state has become unaffordable.
   2. Society as a whole of social relations threatens to fall apart. A sub class is forming.
   3. Complex and structural problems are not solved. The effect of assistance and service with regard to these problems is usually small. It is an endless task.
   4. The state has taken a paternalistic attitude and taken on too many responsibilities. Decentralization and deregulation will have to take place. In this citizens should (re)gain their own responsibilities: not consultation but

participation.This is why a revision of the welfare state is necessary. Such a revision will result in a more business-like society: the government wants to 'settle', results are expected, which will be verified.

More and more the government and comprehensive health insurance companies want to negotiate with a business contract partner, who is able to clearly show the output of the financial support. Effectiveness must be verifiable and demonstrable. Not only does the government expect greater efficiency from assistance and service, but also a shift in emphasis, from 'compensation to activation': those who ask for help should be given support without taking over responsibilities, if this is not necessary: help should not be aimed at compensation of deficiencies, but concentrate on activating possibilities. In the new subsidising system an 'established' institute will as such no longer receive a grant. In this system the government wants to pay for 'products'. The government wants a standardisation of the help that is offered, both in quality and quantity. System will be introduced that will make it possible to verify and measure quality and quantity. This means the introduction of a market mechanism and consequently institutions will become competitors.

These developments grow into three coherent trends, as far as assistance and service are concerned:

- *Empowerment*

People and groups should be equipped by assistance and service in the best possible way, so that they may take a full place in society and get/maintain a firm grip on their lives and their existence model.

Consequence of this for the policy on assistance:

* From compensation to activation.
* From care and consultation to participation.
* From deficiency to exploitation of possibilities.
* From growing dependant on assistance and service to learning, through programmes, to be as independent as possible. The client should be equipped to act as a market party. In positions where the client is not or hardly capable to do so, the casemanager will take over this position.

- *Accountability:*

Assistance and service should provide a clear view of how and with what means professionals work towards what goal. In other words being able to account for your actions. Issues with accountability are: .are you able to realize the plans that were set, do you consult the client when determining the output etc. Therefore, accountability is not about ideology (what you want to achieve), but about effect (show how you achieve what you want).

This means you render an account of:

* What objectives are set?
* Which alternatives are there?

* Which methods are used?
* What is the input of the client?
* What is the effect on assistance? To what extent have goals been achieved. Because the settlement takes place on the basis of this information.
* How to improve efficiency?

As a result of accountability the institutions for assistance and service will have to deal with:
* Operating according to protocol
* Registration
* Policy on means

(See also the study by G. van der Laan: 'Legitimationsprobleme in der sozialen Arbeit')

- Feedback
Systematically collecting and reporting those matters you run into as a worker and as an institution providing assistance and service. These statistics are a window for politicians. It is the basis for their choices. Withdrawing governments tend to focus on the regulation of facilities through directives and conditions and not so much on what is happening with regard to content in the area of assistance and service. These directives and conditions are developed on the basis of statistics brought in by the institutions. A consequence of feedback is that institutions have to report back to government and politicians by:
* Operating according to protocol
* Registration
* Pointing out and
* Offering alternatives

Next to empowerment, accountability and feedback, other trends can be found. As early as the beginning of the eighties several social workers and policy makers came to the conclusion that *assistance and care do not or hardly provide (efficient} answers for the Complex problems of client.*. Assistance and care are organised in institutions on the basis of partial problems, disciplines and methods. The institutions are not organised in such a way that they can take the complex demand for help from the client as starting point. Therefore the help that is offered with complex problems is cut up and fragmented. Main point is what is offered by the institutions and not the complex demands of clients.

It was found that:
Creating facilities in order to lessen demands somewhere else, usually means creating new demands without decreasing the demands elsewhere. the substitute does not work.

The lines (first and second line) have become dividing lines. Echelonning is a process of division.
The strict use of the terms first and second line stand in the way of finding and stimulating all kinds of useful forms of care that do not fit exactly into the existing compartments.
The echelonning model finds it hard to deal with people that need long-term care or need care with intervals, sometimes in a clinical setting, or maybe a non-institutional-one, or sometimes at home. The line model is a reference model. It was developed from the treatment perspective and the division of labour within the medical profession group and is used as an organisational model for the entire field. Selection and reference are no more than a corridor through expert hierarchy.

On the other hand however, among other things, it has been established that:
- Starting point should' not be persons, disciplines or institutions, but the kind of help that is required (functional construction: care functions)
- Facilities and social workers that have the same objective are considered as one (a function)
  Arrangement according to function provides more possibilities for a cut and dried answer (care made to measure) and increases flexibility.

On the basis of these findings several radical changes are taking place in assistance and care in the early nineties. These changes are based on the conviction that co-operation between different welfare agencies and disciplines is necessary with complex or long-term problems. This co-operation should lead to the co-ordination of care/assistance around one client or client system. This co-ordination of care/assistance (case management) is essential, if the social worker wants to work more efficiently and with a better result.
In connection with these facts the government promotes an extreme co-operation between institutions, by attaching to this co-operation conditions concerning subsidising: the aim is a differentiated offer of assistance by similar facilities, rather than differentiation between facilities 'on the basis of specialised categories. This should lead to a change in the financial facilities that are classified according to category and to sector.
It is particularly important for assistance and care to perceive that the government emphasises the demands (what does the client want), against the one-sided concentration on the facilities that are offered. This means that assistance must come to other forms of help, as well as a different and more intensive form of co-operation.
The main shift that is made in this train of thought, can be summarised as follows:

NOT THE OFFER, NOT THE METHOD, NOT THE DISCIPLINE, NOT THE INSTITUTION IS THE MAIN POINT, BUT THE DEMANDS OF THE CLIENT.

This fundamentally different starting point implies, among other firings:

- Help made to measure. Integral assistance (with complex problems). Organisation of the assistance: case management (with complex problems) An approach concentrating on the client The client as a market party, (specifically in cases of a client-related budget): competition

II Start of the co-operation between the 'Fachhochschule Frankfurt, Abteilung Sozialpädagogik' and the 'Hogeschool van Amsterdam Produktgroep Methodiekontwikkeling'

Both educational schemes have been in contact for over more than 15 years. This contact dates back to the time that the Netherlands, especially to Germany, had the reputation of a paradise for social work and social tourism was the order of the day there. In other words contacts were made particularly through study tours by German students and their teachers - Gerd Gehrmann and Klaus Müller - to Amsterdam. Meanwhile these contacts have changed, intensified:

- Students may study for a given period at the partner-education.
- This year we organised - together with Stockholm - the first joint intensive programme with students from three different countries, the theme of which is: 'Working with families'.
- And we have come together as colleagues, willing to jointly face the challenge of the outlined developments.

In 1991 we have drawn up a 'concept for a European research project for the development of models for consideration of professional methods of social work'.
With regard to content we want to achieve mainly two goals with this project - in co-operation with relevant partners from social work practice in Germany and the Netherlands - being:

- Overcoming the accent on ideology of social work that was done in the seventies and come to a practice theory that may stimulate the actions of social workers.
- And overcoming the - usually therapeutically oriented - concepts and methods for social work practice.

These concepts concentrated on: the individual, his/her problems and a confidential relationship with the worker, a relationship that was described as an instrument for social work. Today I should like to add to this: concepts and methods aimed at compensation. We were looking for concepts and methods in which people are activated, in which people, as active beings, are taken seriously and in which people can be seen in and with their environment, where they look for support, and in which the main issue is the participation of people in social life. For this purpose we wanted to develop methods to reflect and change the professional action of social workers systematically, both in practice and in training.
First we applied for an Erasmus grant for our project. After the initial positive

sounds from Brussels, our 'nice plan' was not eligible for a grant. Verbally we were given to understand that we applied ourselves too strongly to the practice of social work and not enough to the vocational education! Meanwhile our colleagues from Frankfurt - Gerd Gehrmann and Klaus Müller - have published several papers, all concentrated on the reflection of professional action by social workers and on 'Environment Activierungsmethoden'. In Amsterdam, Anjo van Hout and I have described this activating incentive - stimulated by the 'ecological perspectives for social work' from the United States - for social work with youths and particularly those from ethnic groups. Mutual support and stimulation by the educational schemes played an important part in this. Mutual guest lectures provide us with an update on the results of both our work on the one hand, and on the other they root the co-operation within our faculties, both in Frankfurt and Amsterdam. The same development is going to grow with the Stockholm Sociahögskolan - the co-operation partner of the Frankfurt School of Social Work - which became a partner in the described Erasmus-project.

III. Expanding co-operation with the 'Stockholm Universitet Socialhögskolan and the new plans.

After the rejection of our project by Erasmus the co-operation between the three partner educational schemes did not stop. Especially the co-operation between Stockholm Universitet Socialhögskolan was intensified, with Mait Widmark and Thomas Linstein. There is a lot of research taking place at the Socialhögskolan in connection with the graduation programme, as well as in the area of contract activities.

In December 1992, in Frankfurt, the three partners have agreed:

- We will continue to co-operate in the fields of research and methodology development.
- The three higher educational schemes will concentrate research and methodology development on environment programmes and activating programmes.
- In the fall of 1993 we will take a provisional inventory and draw up a concrete plan of action for the following years.
- We will continue to try to acquire a grant from European funds to this effect.

IV. Implementation of the results of international co-operation in the programmes, curricula for social work studies.

Finally I would like to make the following statements concerning international co-operation, which will lead to a number of suggestions for implementations in the curricula for social work studies:

- The developments that were outlined in the introduction, in the fields of policy, organisation and methodology of social work constitute both a great and a difficult challenge for all higher education.
- International co-operation may stimulate the work on this challenge. International acquisition of knowledge and experience may improve the quality of working on innovation.
- Profiling and professionalising- of the practice of social work are the responsibility of all higher educational schemes. The development of instruments for reflection of the professional actions of social workers within a specific policy-wise and organisational context can only be of service to us. After all rendering services on a contract basis is a general development.
- The knowledge and experience we have acquired in the field of research and methodology development, should also be implemented in our social work educational schemes. However this transfer does not take place without problems.
- We may benefit mutually if we jointly develop instruments to evaluate and reflect education for social work in the light of current developments. For it is our final goal to realise truly innovative educational schemes for social work. And for this purpose investments must be made.

Finally, in view of the theme of this colloquium: Social Work and Social Work Studies - Co-operation in Europe 2000 - I think it is meaningful to re-evaluate our international co-operation. I think we should do so on the basis of the following question: 'Do our international contacts stimulate and improve the innovation of our research practice and educational practice for social work?' Or should we say with Quentin Crisp: 'Just weed in your social garden!'

1.2 Ironic Investigations: The Relationship Between Trans-National European Social Work Research and Social Work Education

Andrew Cooper & John Pitts

The Centre for Comparative Social Work Studies [West London Institute, Brunel University]

> "The opposite of irony is common sense. For that is the watchword of those who unselfconsciously describe everything important in terms of the final vocabulary to which they and those around them are habituated. To be commonsensical is to take for granted that statements formulated in that final vocabulary suffice to describe and judge the beliefs, actions and lives of those who employ alternative final vocabularies."

Richard Rorty [1989] Contingency, Irony and Solidarity [p.74]

We believe that people in different countries think in different ways. For example, it seems to us that, despite seine contrary evidence, and at the risk of over-simplifying a complex social reality, people in France, Britain and the United States approach personal and social problems in quite distinct ways. We think that in a problematic situation:

The British tend to ask WHAT questions,
Americans tend to ask HOW questions and
The French tend to ask WHY questions.

This belief is central to our current research and we arrived at itby reading detective stories.

Consider for a moment the ways 'in which Sherlock Holmes, Philip Marlowe and Inspector Maigret conduct their investigations. Sherlock Holmes, a WHAT problem-solver is explaining to his friend Watson the way he solves his cases.

> "To carry the art however to its highest pitch, it is necessary that the reasoner should be able to use all the facts which have come to his knowledge, and this implies, as you will readily see, a possession of all knowledge, which, even in these days of free education and encyclopaedias, is a somewhat rare accomplishment." ..... "a man should keep his little brain attic stocked with all the furniture that he is likely to use and the rest he can put away in the lumber room of his library, where he can get it if he wants"

For Holmes, crime is an intellectual puzzle. By a dazzling display of his powers of deduction Holmes establishes WHAT the facts are. These facts lead him inexorably towards the truth.

For Philip Marlowe, crime is a practical problem. This HOW problem solver, is a

pragmatist, a fixer, he bluffs, follows hunches, and fights and shoots his way through an opaque, dog-eat-dog world in his attempt to get the job done, and to retain a shred of personal integrity
at the same time. In a rare moment of ironic self-examination he describes himself thus:

> "I'm a very smart guy, I haven't a feeling or a scruple in the world. All I have the itch for is money. I am so greedy that for twenty-five bucks a day and expenses, mostly gasoline and whisky, I do my thinking myself, what there is of it; I risk my whole future, the hatred of the cops and of Eddie Mars and his pals, I dodge bullets and eat saps, and say thank you very much, if you have any more trouble, I hope you'll think of me, I'll just leave one of my cards case anything comes up. I do all this for twenty-five bucks a day."

For Maigret, crime is a socio-psychological and existential problem. Like Holmes he deduces facts. Like Marlowe he bluffs and has hunches; but he does something else as well.

> "There comes a time in the course of an investigation," Lucas had said, "when the patron suddenly swells up like a sponge. You'd think he was filling up."
> "But filling up with what? At present, for instance, he was absorbing the fog and the darkness. The village round him was not just any old village. And he was not merely someone who had been cast into these surroundings by chance.
> "He was rather like God the Father. He knew this village like the beck of his hand. It was as if he had always lived here, or better still, as if he had created the little town.. He knew what went on inside all those small, low houses nestling in the darkness."

Holmes inspiration comes from his head, Marlowe's from his 'guts', but when Maigret goes into sponge mode he is engaged in a peculiarly French, possibly peculiarly European, mode of problem-solving; the WHY mode.
We suggest that these three different approaches to problem-solving are not simply a product of the stylistic differences between the authors of detective novels, but drive from culturally specific intellectual traditions, or metaperspectives. The Anglo-French research project which we discuss later in this pamper, transpired to be an engagement with cultural specifics, the problem of elaborating a further metaperspective to encompass differences, and the thus an exercise in methodological invention.

British WHAT Questions

British philosophers from Bacon via Hume to Berkeley, Bentham, Locke Russell and beyond have been preoccupied with gathering empirical evidence to prove whether anything, including themselves, exists. Having had such trouble proving the existence of things which they can see, they are understandably reluctant to grant an existence to things which they cannot see. As a result, the mainstream of British intellectual life has been concerned with the exhaustive naming and cataloguing of phenomena.

Orthodox British psychology is a prime example of this tendency. Traditionally, it has confined itself to the measurement and description of behaviour rather than an explanation of it. One of the consequences of this has been that it has offered us a great deal of information about routine interactions between rats but failed completely to cast any light on the more interesting, but immeasurable, things which human beings do.

While mainstream British philosophy contents itself with an unending discussion about what, if any, relationship exists between objects in the world and the words used to describe them and psychologist stay up all night to discover what time rats eat breakfast, the finest minds in the British legal establishment spend their lives attempting to anticipate what, in any given set of circumstances the hypothetical man "on the .top of the Clapham omnibus" might do.

In the 1950s, Kurt Lewin, a pioneer of group dynamic theory was the leading light among a group of American social scientists who strove to devise a technology for the resolution of social conflict. Their studies of leadership styles and attitude formation, work cultures and productivity, political regimes and social conflict were, first and foremost, about making America work, politically, socially and commercially

In his book, Social Amnesia Jacoby identifies how, in a similarly pragmatic way, American psychology and psychiatry have appropriated Freud, abandoning his radical social critique and hijacking his psychotherapy as a tool with which to keep America normal. Examples of American Can-do-ism are endless. It is a tradition of pragmatic short-term problem-solving in which ideas are adopted and evaluated on the basis of their contribution to the achievement of specific targets.

In a recent radio programme, Laurie Taylor, an English sociologist, remarked that in teaching sociology, unless one adopted a lot of non-English words and concepts, he could only offer the most bland and trivial account of the social world; that certain ways of thinking would not be possible without importing some European concepts.

Durkheim's notion of the Conscience Collective, for example, is remarkably un-British in suggesting that moral decisions are informed by a commonly held set of norms constructed within cultures, rather than a simple process of individual calculation. Subsequently the Frankfurt School brought together psychoanalysis and social theory in an attempt to understand the subtle interplay between social structure, culture and individual biography. Latterly, the late Michel Foucault chronicled in his History of Sexuality the ways in which particular constellations of power come to generate ideologies of normality. But these are just three examples derived from a WHY intellectual tradition which can be traced back to the European enlightenment.

In this paper we want to suggest that these different intellectual traditions have generated different epistemologies, culturally specific metaperspectives, which inform the ways in which we approach, and attempt to gain knowledge about the social phenomena we confront. We argue that in both comparative research and professional education, the major task, and a precondition to understanding, is to find ways of transcending,, or breaking out of, our own "metaperspectives", our ontological and epistemological ghettos, in order to gain an appreciation of what the world looks like from inside a different one.

This is by no means easy however because these metaperspectives, or ontologies, are constructed from historical, cultural, political and socio-structural elements which structure both our inner and outer worlds and constitute our ethnicity.

These metaperspectives are not concepts with which we think but categories of thought, in a near Kantian sense, which structure our conceptual universes and supply a specific vocabulary of meanings. They are not thoughts, but the hidden forces which structure our thinking and to that extent, we are inevitably ethnocentric. Our ethnocentricity is encapsulated and expressed in what Rorty describes as our final vocabulary.

> "It is final in the sense that if doubt is cast on the worth of these words their user has no non-circular argumentative recourse."

.... No option but to keep reiterating their faith in:

> "Christ ', England', 'professional standards ', 'decency ', ' kindness ', ' the Revolution ', ' the Church ', ' progressive ', 'rigorous' 'creative'. The more parochial terms do most of the work." [p73]

In Contingency Irony and Solidarity [1989], Richard Rorty, acknowledging the inevitability of ethnocentricity, takes on the question of whether such ethnocentricity is also inescapable.

We would argue that his answer to this question offers us a sketch of both a necessary attitude for those engaged in comparative transnational research in the applied social sciences and a central, and increasingly important, goal for contemporary professional social work education in Europe.

Rorty commends an attitude of ,irony and suggests that we should strive to become ironists.

This ironist has three characteristics:

1. They have serious doubts about the capacity of their own final vocabulary to make sense of the experience of people with a different final vocabulary.
2. They realise that arguments phrased in their own final vocabulary can neither support or dissolve these doubts - and
3. They do not believe that their final vocabulary offers them a chance of gaining a better grasp of reality or that it has some peculiar hotline to the truth.

Rorty writes:
"I call these people ironists because . . . their renunciation of the attempt to formulate criteria of choice between final vocabularies puts them in the position which Sartre called "metastable": never quite able to take themselves seriously because always aware that the terms in which they describe themselves are subject to change, always aware of the contingency and fragility of their final vocabularies." [pp.73-74]

As we will argue below that, perhaps paradoxically, this stance, rather than promoting a collapse into nihilism or relativism, is a prerequisite for effective social research and social intervention in the multi-national, multi-racial and multi-cultural world of contemporary Europe.

The Doubletake

Writing about the vicious circles and closed systems of the English child protection system and its practices, the endlessly repeating cycle of blame, guilt, and defensive practice, Michael Preston-Shoot and Dick Agass observe how

> ...social work has become involved in a 'game without end' where the now urgent need is to communicate about the communication, to assume a meta position and focus on the system (p 115)

Our experience of comparative research into the French and English systems of child protection-unwittingly but inevitably led us to adopt the meta position advocated here. We came to call it 'doing a doubletake', an experience similar to seeing oneself through the eyes of another person, and realising that 'things really could be different'. Unknowingly, we had in fact incorporated this process at the heart of our research methodology. How did we do this? What did we find? How might it alter our understanding and practice? What kind of new vision unfolds as a consequence?

We believe that in the answers to these questions lie not just local solutions to tensions and struggles in social work practice, but also, through the negotiation of difficult conceptual questions about difference, sameness and power, the possibility of understanding how European identity might itself be forged.

When we look at another country's social work system what do we see? The answer depends partly on the degree of similarity or difference between observer and observed. In Britain, possibly by contrast with continental Europe, there has been a tendency towards convergence and a search for similarity and equivalence in cross-national social work research, the majority of which has involved comparative study among the anglophone countries; the welfare systems of these nations are often historically related, and this tendency is reinforced by the mobility of English speaking labour and mutually reinforcing research endeavours. But in the end only a narcissist sees the value of looking at himself in the mirror all the time; the more he looks the more he sees only himself, and the more terrifying and inconceivable becomes the possibility of seeing any one else. What then remains to support us against incomprehension, confusion and the narcissistic wounding of our ethnocentricity when we cross real frontiers of language, culture, history and ideology in the pursuit of knowledge?

One answer, and we believe in its simple form a mistaken one, would be 'our methedologies'. In this respect we will illustrate an early lesson in disillusionment from our research. We had set out on a pilot project to compare the social work roles in French and English child protection work. Representative groups of workers from each country would answer individual questionnaires about a case study, then hold videoed discussions about how they would proceed within their respective systems, and we and the workers would compare national responses. We sat down with our French colleagues to design the case study, sharing a common intention to base this on a real case in one or other country. Impossible. Why? Because the two systems are so different that the development of any case in either country quickly assumes features which are unrecognisable in the other. We tried a hypothetical case based on work in one country. Same problem. In the end we found that while we could design a study which was neutral with respect to both systems, it had to be entirely stripped bare of references to institutional, organisational, cultural and professional factors.

Our first lesson in methodology was learned in the futile attempt to apply a familiar, tried and tested methodology, and find it wanting. Ordinarily the case study approach sits on a submerged iceberg of cultural, professional and .philosophical assumptions. In its own waters it can do so undisturbed. In foreign ones, where the cultural temperature is different it may melt rapidly. A case study, to paraphrase Rorty, still tries to hold a mirror up to nature, to imitate, to simulate. In its own country, while it may not be the 'real thing' it will reflect faithfully enough. But across the national frontier 'nature' is different, and the mirror clouds over and distorts.

How then did our research participants proceed? In each country, our groups of workers responded to the case study, completed their questionnaires and held videoed discussions about the case; these discussions were then dubbed into the other language, shown to the groups in the other country who were asked to comment on 'What's the same and what's different about your colleagues handling of the case?' And here we discovered a new, more complex validity to the mirror metaphor. Instead of seeing only sameness or difference, only their own system and practices or the other, participants saw both simultaneously.

Each question and each answer came to have a double information load. We will illustrate this with a simple example.

In England it is necessary to gather legally admissible evidence of child abuse before a child protection case can be brought into the legal arena. In France this is not so; a social worker can refer a family or child to the Children's Judge without 'proof' of abuse, and in contrast to England again, may do so precisely because the parents are uncooperative in providing it. Consequently, in our study English workers referred frequently to questions of evidence and proof, as a condition of the possibility of further action on the case, while their French counterparts made no mention of equivalent concepts. On viewing the French discussions, English workers asked two types of question - 'The French workers didn't discuss evidence at all, I wonder what that says about their system?' but also 'We spoke about evidence a lot, what does that say about our system?' In both statements, the silent implication is 'By comparison with...'

When we look at another country's social work system, our own appears in the conceptual spaces and apparent lacunae of the other, and theirs in the hitherto unidentified, unseeable spaces surrounding our own. These spaces represent the possibility of difference, change. To change yourself you must first see yourself differently, as a being with possibilities; the final vocabulary which is the ground of your identity transpires to be a misrecognition of the permanence of the self, a reflection of social identity.

> ...only by being reflected in another man - that is, in so far as this other man offers it an image of its unity - can the ego arrive at its self-identity; identity and alienation are thus strictly correlative. (Zizek, 1989, p 24)

Something else of great importance is implied by our initial struggle with the writing of the case study. Stripped of all references to the professional and cultural practices. of each country, and yet still meaningful to the practitioners of each, what did this residuum amount to? Ostensibly a kind of 'core' description of social behaviour ('worrying child care practice') con, non to each nation, a bridge, a point of contact beyond differences. Operationally this may have been true; the practitioners in both countries could work with this material. But as our work progressed we realised that even this certainty had to be relinquished. Let's return to the question of evidence.

In England the search for evidence of child abuse as a precondition of access to the legal arena, is linked to the need to prove a case in court; court proceedings in turn take an adversarial form in which lawyers, social workers, experts, and to a limited degree children and families, engage in a formalised battle to establish guilt or innocence. These words 'guilt' and 'innocence' are not actually used, but anyone unfortunate enough to have been an actor in one of these legal dramas knows that these are just what is at stake. Evidence, proof, guilt and innocence - we posit these as part of the final vocabulary of English child care social work. In France, because legal child care proceedings are conducted in an inquisitorial framework, without reference to concepts of guilt and innocence, but more in the spirit of a search for understanding about the suffering of the child and her or his family, social workers undertaking an assessment are not gathering evidence, but information. Their final vocabulary is different - information, understanding and suffering. Note that these vocabularies do not consist of isolated, randomly associated words or concepts; they are systems of meaning, in which each term finds its place by reference to, and connection with, other discursively compatible terms. They are internally consistent vocabularies.

When social workers go about their tasks in France and England, let's say a child protection assessment, they might appear to a naive investigator to be doing very similar things; they ask the same sorts of people the same sorts of questions, and much of the time would seem to worry about similar kinds of things. But this similitude is illusory in our view. The mirror is lying again. Its images disclose behaviour, but not so the meanings embedded within it, and which partly constitute it. It is our thesis that because of the cultural, ideological and discursive embeddedness of even mundane social work practices, there is no necessary equivalence between two apparently similar professional behaviours in two nations. Just as the various elements of a vocabulary derive their meaning from their internal relatedness, so do the elements of social, and social work, practice.

At this point you may ask 'How then can we ever understand another social work system? It seems in your view to be a discursively closed phenomena. How do you enter it?' It is a good question, and to contemporary epistemologists since Wittgenstein, a familiar one. Our answer is 'Not through any ordinary door or window; perhaps more like through a skylight in the roof'. We said earlier that the 'final vocabularies' with which we are concerned are akin to Kantian categories; they are the ground of the possibility of thinking, intersubjectivity, and cultural practice itself; thus fortunately, most of the time in everyday life they do not bother us, but are taken for granted. They are there precisely so that we don't have to think too much about what we mean when we communicate; so that when we say something we just mean it, and when we do something others know what we mean by what we do. But in our situation this no longer suffices. However, it is the uniquely human capacity to think about thinking which renders possible our entry to another world where 'they think things differently'. So in our research we have found that we must struggle not just with 'language difficulties' as the tourist or traveller must, but with thinking itself. We have become barefoot philosophers, constantly disinterring presuppositions we did not know we had, in order to properly explain ourselves, and listening to our French colleagues do the same so-we could understand our failures to understand them. We often wondered why we returned from our trips to France so comprehensively exhausted.

So far we have concentrated on 'the problems and revelations of understanding everday social work practice in another country. On the whole these aspects of the research focus, while effortful, were uncontentious. It was not always so. Social work itself is always bound up with the character of the total society of which it is a pert. Inevitably then our research drew us into engagement with political philosophy, and in particular the deep and divergent historic roots of our two societies. Here we sometimes encountered limits to our own capacity for relativism, understanding, and non-judgmental enquiry.

It seems to us that English political and social work culture is blindly wedded to a philosophy of rights, and especially the rights of the individual. Elsewhere (Cooper at al 1992) we have argued that our newest legislation, the Children Act, can be seen as an attempt to resolve persistent problems of conflicts of rights between parents and children, by assigning yet more rights to more categories of individuals. Here and there, it is true that people's duties also make an appearance in this discourse, but not in a way which assumes they have a fundamental relationship with people's rights. This subordination of duties to rights is a characteristically liberal stance.

A French colleague said to us recently 'French republicanism is not liberalism; at the heart of the social contract which the Republic embodies are certain absolutes'. And to English consciousness it can be astonishing to hear a French Children's Judge citing the Civil or Family Code in his or her direct dealings with a family - codes which derive directly from the French constitution and state the rights and duties of parents and children; or to hear one of the French social workers in our study, talking about the question of cultural difference in child protection work with North African families, say 'From the moment that these people arrive in France they have to be warned of their rights and duties, that there are laws to be respected...certainly this kind of thing makes our understanding of a case more complicated, but for myself, it's true, I say in France there are French laws.' In England we tend to hear this as pure, unreconstructed post-imperialist arrogance. Very illiberal; such matters should be the subject of negotiation, accommodation, respect for difference, we say. But in England, by contrast with France, the state offers no definite, constitutionally defined guarantees to individuals in return for the demand of obeisance to the law. Thus in England today, the majority of black social workers or students will say that they are first and foremost - black. In Britain the realities of racism have pushed black people and their communities inexorably towards staking a claim to civil and legal rights as black people. We are not suggesting that the realities of racism are necessarily any less acute in France, but in our limited experience, 'black' social workers and students in France, want first and foremost to identify and claim their rights as French citizens. Thus one near equivalent to British 'anti-racism', the movement SOS Racism, aspires to greater integration as a political ideal. It is tempting to us as English observers to say 'They are twenty years behind us', but we believe the truth is actually harder to bear; we are different, and have different histories, different identities, and different final vocabularies of political possibility.

The point was graphically illustrated in a recent article in the Women's section of the British newspaper The Guardian (3.3.93)

'In a Paris park in 1987, a Gambian woman met another African woman who offered to cut out her daughter's clitoris with a knife...she would pay more than £42 for the clitoral excisions; however six years later she would pay with a year in prison...Although there have been no prosecutions under UK child abuse laws, health workers fear that 10,000 children are at risk of being excised...many African women were outraged by calls last month from Kenyan born Poline Nyaga of London's Brent Council to legalise female circumcision. According to Nyaga..."Circumcision should be allowed as a right to all British women, particularly for African families who want to carry on their traditions while living in this country". The headline of this article asked 'What is Europe doing about female circumcision?' The question, in our view, lacks sufficient irony. Which Europe, who's Europe, Europe...what is Europe? We do not propose that asking questions about questions is always and everywhere an answer. We do not have an answer, but we do believe our experiences have shown us the importance of asking the right questions. If anything we ourselves are less the English liberal and more the republican absolutist. But the encounter in our research with the reflexive complexity of national differences has faced us with the dilemma encapsulated in the contemporary debate between the modernists and the post-modernists - do we- abandon all searches for a grand narrative of social existence in Europe, recognising that the only certainty is of never finding certainty? Or do we acknowledge plurality, difference, tension, incompatibility, but still seek to ground our practices (social work and others) in some working value consensus about difference?What we can formulate is a set of current aspirations for cross national social work education and research in Europe, which reflect the complexities we have articulated in this paper.

Thus, in our research and student exchanges we are trying to:

1 Render the familiar-unfamiliar
2 Promote the perception of differences and the attempt to understand them in their socio-historical-cultural specificity.
3 Jettison our existing culturally specific compasses, come to terms with the loss of 'equivalence' as a meaningful category in social research; and so embrace the need to recontextualise phenomena, even relatively familiar phenomena, which leads to a need to understand the new context. The pursuit of equivalence is fruitless because of the historico-cultural-political specifity of cross-national divisions
4 This context is historical/ political/ socio-structural/ cultural-linguistic/ intellectual-theoretical
5 To grasp this requires a capacity for, and a commitment to, abstraction, to thinking about thinking. The adoption and adaptation of agreed second-order constructs which can encapsulate the different experiences.
6 Like being in love, cross national research cannot be learned about by reading books or sitting alone in an office poring over data. It must be experienced to yield understanding and meaning. That is why we believe that all such research must be participant research.
7 We aim to enable people to think in a plurality of vocabularies and this it seems to us is a pre-requisite of being European - not simply to understand the laws and and formal structures which describe the services, not this unending search

> for equivalence but a capacity to transcend ethnocentricity, to suspend, or place in parantheses, one's conceptual vocabulary of origin and take on another and then, the mark of real pluralism, to be able to hold both - side by side, without judging or evaluating them and comparing there without lapsing into the pursuit of equivalences.

But do we do this simply to promote a new form of non-ethnocentric, non-xenophobic, pluralistic, Euro-speak in which we can express respect for one another's traditions. We would argue that, as a first step, the attempt at understanding is important but that we are not ultimately simply concerned with a greater understanding of what is. If the only challenge we faced concerned communications between relatively prosperous relatively secure western European academics and welfare professionals we would be very happy.

Rather, we are concerned with the development of a capacity and a means of understanding people, cultures and systems different from our own. Behind the facade of a prosperous white Western European Community is the reality of a relatively impoverished Afro-Carribean, Arabic, Asian, Islamic and Slavic Europe. These are the people who, increasingly, make up the caseloads of welfare professionals in the EC. Social scientists and social work educators who wish to retain some relevance to practice in welfare systems, must devise ways of understanding and reaching these marginalised Europeans. They need to avoid the fate of American academics whom, as Edward Said [1993] observes have been swallowed up by the state and by the professionalisation of academic life. Hew rites:

"Cults like post-modernism, discourse analysis, New Historicism, deconstruction, neo-pragmatism transport them into the country of the blue; an astonishing sense of weightlessness with regard to the gravity of history and individual responsibility fritters away attention to public matters and public discourse. The result is a kind of floundering about that is most dispiriting to witness, even as the society as a whole drifts without direction or coherence. Racism, poverty, ecological ravages disease and an appallingly widespread ignorance: these are left to the media and the odd political candidate during an election campaign." [p367]

1.3 An Ettiquette for Social Workers

Geert van der Laan

In the 1980s social work (in the Netherlands) ran the gauntlet between two rows of critics. The advocates of a businesslike, market-oriented approach in the welfare sector (neo-conservatism) argued that, instead of adopting a communicative attitude, social workers should turn out concrete products which social services could use as a strategic instrument to compete with other services. But before social workers got the chance to consider the choice between a communicative and a strategic action model, the critics, following the French philosopher Foucault (postmodernism), had already made clear that this choice was 'an illusion of alternatives' by demonstrating that all too often a communicative attitude Is used to mask power and disciplinary strategies.

Thus the critics always had a stick to beat the dog. No matter what social workers did, the outside world was seldom pleased.

Now that the nineties have been heralded by an appeal from the Dutch Government for social renewal, it has become particularly important to consider what legitimisation social workers can offer for their actions in situations of social disadvantage. Because of the increasing number of complex care demands, resulting from phenomena such as extra-muralisation and marginalization, the legitimisation problem is relevant primarily to professional dilemmas the average social worker cannot resolve easily. I am referring to matters concerning neglect, poverty, social instability, violence, addiction, major family conflicts, and the like. If the criticism directed against social work is to contribute towards improving the quality of these services, it will have to hold out the prospect of a more effective approach of the hard core of complex care demands social workers are confronted with.

Prudent care

What procedures are available to assess the quality of social workers' actions in order to establish whether and to what extent the massive criticism of this kind of work is justified?

The simplest procedure would be discussing social workers' actions before a (hypothetical) jury, consisting of (representatives of) clients, colleagues, subsidizers and the public. In that case a social worker's professional obligation to legitimate his actions in a specific case would imply that he must be able to demonstrate that he has acted prudently, on the strength of his competence as a trained social worker, and in accordance with the established professional standards of social work.

-The concept of 'prudent care' has been brought to the attention of social services by legal discussions about the policy adopted by various Dutch 'young people's advisory centres' to enable children who have run away from home to escape parental authority. At present a social worker involved in such a case will not be prosecuted if the advisory centre can show that the support offered to the child meets the criteria of prudent care. In practice this means that the parents or guardian are contacted as soon as possible; that they are allowed to participate in the care process; that the social worker examines whether the child welfare office should be involved; that the social worker acts in accordance with his professional code; and that his actions remain verifiable.

In doubtful cases it is the responsibility of the juvenile court to determine afterwards whether the workers involved have acted prudently. These criteria barely reflect on the content of the care process, i.e. the way in which the child's problem has been dealt with. This is what the criteria of prudent care should in fact be based on.

The problem social workers are faced with, however, is that as far as content is concerned it is difficult to draw up 'protocols', as is done in some fields of medicine, that are based on reasonably well-founded empirical-statistic knowledge of connections between causes and symptoms. This is what makes standardising social work as a 'businesslike product' so difficult.

Mooij (1989) uses the term 'prudence' to refer to the moral domain which in concrete, unsettled matters should be assessed correctly before a sensible decision can be made. Mooij emphasises that 'prudence' pertains, not to the automatic application of previously acquired insights, but to a personal insight based on an accurate sense of proportion and good judgement. The question is whether it is possible to give social workers something more to catch on to than deliberately vague terms such as 'moral domain', 'sense of proportion' and 'good judgement'. Social work has after all been criticised particularly for its vagueness.

Three criteria

For a quality assessment of social workers' actions I would like to advance three central criteria:

- the resolution of the 'reduction problem';
- the quality of the communication;
- the legitimisation of intervention and/or non intervention.

These criteria are by no means exhaustive, but are brought forward to counterbalance the two earlier-mentioned forms of criticism of social work, and consequently are intended to answer two questions:

- Does social work have the capacity to define itself as a business-like product?
- Does social work have the capacity to avoid patronising and disciplinary practices?

To illustrate the practical significance of these questions, I will discuss one of the dilemmas social workers can be confronted with.

The authenticity of care demands

One day a social service is approached by a woman, we will call her Mrs Janssen, who wishes to know whether she can talk to a social worker on a regular basis, if

need be about the weather. She has discovered that her husband will stop battering her if he knows that she has contacted an official agency, possibly because then he will feel that he is under some kind of surveillance. Mrs Janssen states that she does not want to divorce her husband as long as their children are still living at home.
This concrete client demand places the social worker in a dilemma: should she 'simply' acknowledge Mrs Janssen's responsibility for her own decisions, or should she (apply the methods she has at her disposal to) induce her client to take her own interest at heart and leave her husband?
By .means of this example we can also ask ourselves in what respect the criticism of social work in the eighties holds out the prospect of improved methodic action. Is the customer always right? To what extent can social work be looked upon as a product? Is it the task of the social worker to satisfy the 'customer'? What does emancipation mean in this case, and what choice would lead to paternalism? Where does (female) solidarity from the social movement end and do professional considerations begin?
To get a grip on these' matters I will briefly examine the alternatives that are available to social services in these kinds of cases. Then it will be possible to determine the extent to which the professional responsibility of this kind of work can be made procedurally verifiable and the methodology managerially regulated and standardised.
From a strictly (methodo)logical point of view the social worker can make two different errors:
- error type 1: intervene unjustly;
- error type 2: unjustly not intervene.

The first type of error can be associated with terms such as 'patronisation', 'paternalism' and 'disciplinary techniques'; the second error with 'negligence', as it is called in the medical profession. 'Patronisation' implies that a person is unjustly deprived of his power of decision. 'Negligence' means that a worker evades his professional responsibilities.
A curious aspect of this distinction is that efforts towards avoiding one type of error automatically increase the risk of making the other type of error. By never intervening, workers can avoid error type 1, but the risk of making error type 2 will then increase accordingly, and vice versa. In the Bolderkar affair[1] workers decided to eliminate error 2 through unrestrained intervention. As a result the public got the impression that workers did not act prudently and lapsed into error 1.
Both kinds of error, unjust intervention and negligence, can only be avoided by a careful assessment of each individual case. What is right in one case can be wrong in another. The professional standards by which prudent care is judged should, however, be formulated in such a way that both types of error can be brought up for discussion. How does this correspond to the disciplinary rules of social work?

Disciplinary rules and supervision

In 1977 a social worker was reprimanded by the Supervisory Board of the Dutch Association of Social Workers, because he had helped a client find a secret address where she could escape her husband's abuse[2]. The reprimand was based on a formal, procedural argument: the worker involved had maintained a professional worker-client relationship with both spouses, and had then taken sides. Not an assessment of the serious nature of the situation was the deciding factor for the board, but the formal correctness of the worker's actions.

This example, like the advisory centre case, reveals a certain preoccupation with the procedural aspects of social work and the avoidance of error type 1. Although disciplinary measures are not a prominent feature of the welfare sector, it seems that in social work - in contrast to the medical profession - unjust intervention is generally considered to be a more serious error than negligence. We may ask ourselves why the disciplinary rules of social work cannot be applied consistently to eliminate both errors.

Mrs Janssen's social worker knows that her client is abused by her husband. Suppose that one ill-fated day her fears prove to be justified: Mrs Janssen is so severely beaten that she does not recover from her injuries. Will the social worker be suspended because of negligence? Will she be considered liable on account of her responsibility for the well-being of a client consigned to her care? Under the present circumstances this is not likely to happen, although it is to be expected that, because of the growing publicity surrounding cases of abuse, public opinion will bring negligent professionals more and more to account. I am referring to publications in the Dutch weekly Vrij Nederland about the death of a foster child. The articles concentrated on the question how three children could be abused for years by their foster parents under the social workers' very eyes without anyone interfering. Even then, however, it will still be extremely difficult to establish in which cases a social worker has acted correctly or incorrectly or, to put it differently, has turned out quality work.

Sorting machine

The discussion concerning both types of error usually involves a 'truth discourse', i.e. a debate about the technical instruments that can be used to determine to what extent a statement about a particular situation in the world can be characterised as 'true' or 'untrue'. In the Bolderkar affair the (public) debate ultimately concentrated on the question whether according to scientifically accepted standards the so-called 'dolls method' was a technically reliable instrument to identify incest victims. Through this • truth discourse' about the quality of social work, a normative discussion about the acceptability of child abuse was more or less pushed into the background.

We are dealing here with a 'reduction problem': the reduction of a wide field of experience to a technical-instrumental aspect.

The reduction problem in the welfare sector can be resolved by means of the three formal world perspectives distinguished by Jürgen Habermas (1981). By putting his 'sorting machine' into operation we can examine whether and to what extent it is possible to unfold various validity claims. In Habermas's view these claims can refer to objective matters (the truth of facts), to social matters (the appropriateness of norms) and to subjective statements (the authenticity of utterances). Analogous to this distinction between objective, social and subjective aspects of the problem situation we can map the corresponding skills. In addition it will be possible to identify the respective fixations on one world. These matters have been related to each other in diagram 1:

Diagram 1: Three worlds

world	**validity claim**	**competence**	**reduction**
objective	truth of facts	instrumental	rationalisation
social	appropriateness of norms	social	moralisation
subjective	authenticity of utterances	expressive	therapeutisation

I will briefly elucidate this diagram by means of an example. Phrase books like Italian for Beginners inevitably contain short sentences such as "Waiter, there's a draught here!" The composers of these kinds of books rightly assume that it is useful to learn such phrases by heart, because they express a lot.

"Waiter, there's a draught here" is (a) a statement about the objective situation, (b) an appeal to a social norm which requires the waiter to act, and (c) the expression of a subjective experience. In everyday life the restaurant guest expects the waiter to close the window, and the waiter understands what the guest expects him to do. If, however, the waiter only responds to the first aspect by saying: "You're right, Sir, there is a draught here", the communication has not been entirely successful, since the guest wanted to lay a claim, not only to the truth of his statement, but also to the normative correctness of his expectation that the-waiter will do something about it, and thirdly to the authenticity of the subjective experience that he is beginning to shiver with cold.

The waiter can accept all three claims, on the .principle that the customer is always right, but he can also dispute them. With regard to the third claim, for instance, he can say: "I beg your pardon, Sir, but I don't feel a draught. Could it be that you're coming down with flu, and that that's why you're shivering?" This kind of discussion is what Habermas calls a Diskurs. Hence we speak of discursive communication when validity claims can be disputed by both communication partners.

These validity claims correspond to different competencies. For instance, the speaker in question must know the rules of conduct of the (sub)culture involved, and be able to express himself in such a way that the listener does not get the impression that he is pretending to be cold. Mirrorwise, these skills also apply to the

her client questions such as: 'What stops you from filing for divorce?' and 'How would you feel if you were on your own?' Kunneman (1986) would call this procedure an 'identity discourse'.
The social worker's report does not reveal to what extent she discusses her own validity claims with her client or her fellow workers. She does however mention a confrontation with her client's husband during one of the talks that took place at the home of the Janssen family: "... he sits down in the middle of the room and demonstratively starts cleaning his fingernails with a knife. I feel uncomfortable."
The effect of these kinds of factors also seems to be important for a quality assessment of the social worker's actions.
According to the worker's report Mrs Janssen keeps to her decision. The worker must therefore decide whether she is willing to accept the risks that are involved in this case. Talking with her client is the only instrument she can use to make this decision. Without reverting to therapeutisation, the social worker will have to create conditions for a dialogue in which Mrs Janssen can freely and safely be 'authentic' or, as Golfman puts it, is given the opportunity to offer a truthful presentation of herself.
If we follow this line of thought we can formulate a second quality criterion to assess whether workers have acted prudently:. communication between worker and client should be dialogical in nature, in the sense that the client's validity claims should be taken seriously within a shared definition of the situation. This does not mean that the claims cannot be discussed. But the latter does not require a transition to an objectifying approach. Workers can act as communication partners and contribute actively to the development of a mutual understanding (Kunneman, 1986). This active approach has the following consequences:

- the other person's statements should be judged on the basis of their validity;
- one's own assessment standards are also put on the line.

This means that the worker enters into a symmetrical relationship and cannot simply assume that his client's views and standards are inferior to his own. The compatibility of such an approach with the principle of professional responsibility will be discussed in the following section. Clear in any case is that a dialogical (communication) model makes it impossible to work according to protocol, in the sense of using a specific decision tree in which professional views and standards are superior to the views and standards of the client, and by means of which the worker only has to categorise the client to find out how he should act.
This 'dialogical' criterion can also be applied to the interaction between workers. An important aspect of group supervision is that workers support each other. In addition critical assessments of professional actions are made. A symptomatic error of the bread and sandals brigade of the sixties and seventies was that all validity claims, of workers as well as clients, were per definition taken as true, justified and above all authentic. Although I do not wish to advocate a return to this situation, I would like to argue in favour of a welfare sector that maintains its 'soft' character and whose workers have the courage to put their own assessment standards on the

line before clients and fellow workers.
Mrs Janssen's care demand requires a specification of the terms 'emancipation' and 'disciplinary techniques'. Although 'disciplinary techniques' have not always been clearly defined, it has justly been associated with power and unilateral manipulation. Disciplinary techniques involves ignoring the other person's validity claims and imposing the worker's truth on the client. By now the point of friction of the power-discussion may have become clear.
In accordance with Foucault and Achterhuis, some theorists tend to ascribe the disciplinary role to the professionals, whereas the social movements are seen as the exclusive vehicle of liberation. I have used the Bolderkar affair as an example to disprove the existence of a permanent, fundamental discrepancy between the emancipation efforts of the social movements and the professions' power of truth. The Bolderkar affair clearly demonstrates how emancipation efforts can gradually be transformed into disciplinary power. The workers of the Bolderkar appeared to be inspired by motives from the social movements rather than by professional considerations of prudent care. In the long run, however, the Bolderkar discourse was reduced to a truth discourse, which created the picture of emancipation-oriented workers whose actions were of a purely instrumental nature. The connection between power and knowledge is therefore not the exclusive monopoly of the oppressors. It is also willingly used by the liberators; indeed as a counter force, but this cannot replace a normative discussion.
Professional workers are personally responsible for their actions on the basis of a normative legitimisation and an independent social position. They should serve neither ruling powers nor opposing forces. There are of course various degrees of independence. So far I have been able to identify three varieties (Van der Laan, 1990): on the one hand, care provided within the context of detention under a restriction order, in which the possibility to take clients' validity claims seriously is structurally restricted; on the other hand, the model of the patient advocate used in psychiatry, who take every validity claim made by clients seriously by virtue of his profession. Interpretation is not necessary. There is no assessment. In fact the patient advocate's approach is extremely simple: take every word the patient says absolutely seriously and act as his counsel.
Between these two extremes there are gradations of independence, for instance within the context of general welfare and rehabilitation services.

Intervention or non-intervention

What has been said in the previous section could lead to the mistaken notion that the dialogue is the alpha and omega of social work. Also in social work, however, as in other social sectors, the dialogue may at a certain point come to an end. A plea for the dialogue as a basic form of social work does not necessarily include a plea for endless discussion. At some stage the dialogue turns into a monologue. That is when the democratic discussion is concluded and a decision is carried out. At that listener.

As a rule, social workers are reasonably well-trained in recognising such skills in clients (and responding adequately to them), although the tendency to therapeutisation within social work focus on the expressive aspects ('what do you feel about a problem?'), while neo-conservatism tends to magnify the objective (or objectifiable) world ('what is the concrete problem?').

Validity claims do not always have to be accepted implicitly. The essence of communicative action is that the validity claims can be disputed. Applied to the welfare sector this means that it is a misunderstanding to think that a communicative approach implies that the worker should indiscriminately adopt the client's self-description. This would be a questionable interpretation of solidarity. Nor does a communicative approach mean that every self-description should be disputed, since this would lead to indecisiveness and would exhaust the life world. It is the possibility to dispute them that is important.

Three worlds

An analysis of Mrs Janssen's care demand in accordance with Diagram 1 leads to the following questions:

World 1 (objective): To what extent have the rights and wrongs of the case become clear? What does the social worker know about the actual situation?

World 2 (social): Is it morally acceptable to leave a woman in a situation in which serious accidents are likely to take place? What are Mrs Janssen's own standards and values? What is considered 'normal' in her milieu?

World 3 (subjective): To what extent is the client's care demand authentic? To what extent is she still subject of her own actions? Has she taken this decision of her own free will or has it been forced upon her by circumstances, in which case she may not be 'fully accountable'?

The social worker will also have to examine her own role as a professional:

World 1: Do social workers have objective methods at their disposal to determine the definite extent of abuse in a specific case? (For instance the 'dolls method', used in the medical day-care centre De Bolderkar.)

World 2: Is it prudent, professionally speaking, to allow oneself to be used as an 'authority' that, in a sense, is kept in reserve to be used as a wild card to stabilise an anything but sound family situation? Should the social worker be held professionally responsible the moment a serious accident takes place?. Can she be brought to account for negligence? Is the social worker allowed to overrule her client's decision? World 3: To what extent are the social worker's own motives authentic? To what extent is a cautious strategy determined by the permanent threat of violence to which she, as a woman, is also susceptible? Where do her professional considerations end and her own fears come in?

A reconstruction of this case (Van der Laan, 1990) shows that the question concerning the authenticity of this client demand is of crucial importance for a quality

assessment of the care' provided. This also means that quality assessments are extremely difficult to substantiate. Workers must be able to stand their ground, not only in a discussion about the truth of facts, but also in a dialogue about the appropriateness of norms and the authenticity of subjective utterances. Particularly in a sector in which a strong appeal is made to the moral and personal dedication of the people involved, the appropriateness of norms as well as the authenticity of subjective statements should not be neglected in worker-client relationships, supervision, team discussions or the development of professional theory.
These considerations point to the first quality criterion of social workers' actions: a worker-client relationship should offer the possibility of a smooth transition between objective, normative and subjective aspects of the problem situation.
Here the accompanying assessment problems are already implied in the criterion itself. The fact is that normative and subjective considerations are inherently difficult to 'objectify' and verify procedurally. In addition this solution of the reduction problem complicates the welfare sector's managerial streamlining process, since the reduction to a measurable product is only part of the problem. It does however meet the criticism expressed by Foucault. By means of Habermas's sorting machine the 'connection between power and knowledge' which frequently occurs in Foucault's criticism of the welfare sector, can be interpreted as the dominance of the truth discourse over normative issues and questions concerning the authenticity of expressions of the personal identity. Within the sorting machine the technical-instrumental aspects of the care situation can be 'shown their place'.

Dialogue

The 'connection of power and-knowledge' does not only refer to the reduction of the reality of social work to objective aspects. It also refers to the way in which the three world aspects and the corresponding validity claims are approached. We can also speak of the 'connection of power and knowledge' when the client's validity claims are influenced. In such cases the term is synonymous with unilateral manipulation. A smooth transition between the three world perspectives is therefore not enough, since this can still serve a strategic action model.
In the Janssen case the social worker's approach to her client's validity claims is at issue. As has been said earlier, it is particularly the authenticity claim that needs to be examined more closely by the social worker. Is the client indeed in control of her own actions or has she been so badly abused that she can no longer be considered capable of making her own decisions? In the latter case the worker is faced with the question whether she may take over responsibility and turn to unilateral manipulation.
The only fact the worker can proceed from Is her client's statement that she does not want to divorce her husband, at least not as long as the children are still living at home. The social worker's work report reveals that she has discussed this decision extensively with her client. She has tried to introduce other options by asking

point the worker stops listening and writes out a prescription.
Consequently, the third quality criterion pertains to the transition from dialogue to monologue, to dealing with the worker's dilemma of intervention or non-intervention.

> To avoid patronising and disciplinary practices, social workers are usually quite reluctant to intervene directly. On the whole they have little faith in going against a client's wishes, because it affects the client's trust and undermines the principle of client autonomy laid down in the professional code. Although the practical implication of this reluctance is that it reduces the risk of intervening unjustly, it also increases the risk of negligence. As has been said earlier, unjust intervention is an error that causes greater commotion within social work than unjust non-intervention. In my view the aggravation of social problems in the eighties indicates that negligence deserves greater attention. The third quality criterion is therefore concerned with the extent to which social workers manage to avoid both errors. The question is, however, whether workers-should be encouraged to eliminate negligence, since this would also stimulate the use of power. I would like to argue that the use of power or professional influence is permissible on the strict condition that it can be legitimated. How can one thing be reconciled with the other?

The problem lies in the definition of what does and what does not belong to the communicative action model. The essence of the model is that the person in question can bring forward good reasons for a particular action, and that these reasons can be discussed, assuming that the other person has the ability to participate in this discussion open-heartedly. In other words the discussion partners should both be fully responsible and communicatively competent. In situations in which the social worker is confronted with abuse, addiction, severe mental illness and the like, these conditions cannot 'always be met. The key-question in such situations is whether the worker should postpone his actions or whether he may intervene provided he discusses his reasons for doing so either beforehand (contract) or afterwards (legitimisation).
A lot of authors hold the view that the client should under no circumstances be subordinated to the worker's truth and aims. We may ask ourselves, however, whether the communicative action model could not function (at a meta-level) within the context of a subsequent legitimisation (afterwards) before (representatives of) the client, the professional group or the public. It is, after all, conceivable that so much trust has developed in a worker-client relationship that the client can authorise the worker beforehand, on well-defined conditions, to arrange hospitalisation, for instance in cases of a threatening psychosis. Such 'contracts' also occur in situations involving euthanasia for which a relationship based on mutual trust, instead of being jeopardised, is an essential prerequisite. Intervention cannot always be legitimated instantly. It often happens that a communicative validation is provided afterwards, or that in precedinq negotiations efforts to arrive at a joint definition of the situation lead to a form of agreement which as a kind of 'meta-communicative

label', for instance during hospitalisation, accompanies the subsequent care process.

Aims and means

For a more detailed analysis of the use of power in care situations I have adopted the distinction Kunneman (1986) makes between:

- the orientation of the actor: communicative or strategic aims and
- the mechanisms of action co-ordination: communicative or strategic means.

With this a subtle distinction can be made between what for convenience's sake I would like to call 'the strategic use of communicative means' and 'the communicative use of strategic means'. This has been represented in Diagram 2:

Diagram 2 Orientation and action co-ordination

form of action co-ordination / orientation of the actor	communicative means	strategic means
communicative aims	1 communicative aims	2 communicative use of strategic means
strategic aims	2 communicative use of strategic means	4 overt strategic action

The flood of critical publications on welfare work in the eighties was concerned with the 'disclosure' of latent strategic action (square 3). Unfortunately, Kunneman has paid no attention to square 2, the communicative use of strategic means. Especially in the welfare sector, however, it is important to examine to what extent strategic means are used in practice to develop rationally justifiable forms of action co-ordination. In care situations a distinction can be made between a meta-level of the definition of the situation and an object-level of the actual care provided. The term 'meta-level' refers to the level at which statements are made about the significance of the action at the original level.

Stratified communication

In accordance with communicative theory it is possible to speak of stratified communication. A single communicative action can consist of various layers which differ according to the type of action; a discrepancy that need not have a damaging effect. Some parents manage to punish their children without making them feel that punishment involves permanent loss of parental love. Apparently a 'label' is attached to the punishment, or a meta-communicative message is conveyed, through attitude or gesture, as a result of which the child is not seized by panic. It is also possible that the child itself knows from experience how to 'label' its parents' anger.

If this is applied to a worker-client relationship, it can be argued that acceptance of the communication's stratification does not mean that a 'double' attitude on the part of the worker has a damaging effect on the client. Particularly in a relationship based on mutual trust it is possible to confront each other directly. This is not the same as the pathogenic double bind to which the Palo Alto school has applied itself, or the latent strategic actions Habermas refers to. Quite the contrary.

Watzlawick et al. have repeatedly pointed out that a specific relationship can be both complementary (inequality) and symmetrical (on equal terms). The two can alternate, but they can also occur simultaneously. A sadomasochistic relationship (if you will excuse the use of such an example in the context of worker-client relationships) is complementary in manifestation, but at a meta-level, where the definition of the situation is negotiated, it can indeed be symmetrical. A relationship does not have to be purely complementary or symmetrical. It can also have both characteristics. The same applies to the famous contrast between emancipation and disciplinary practices. The fact that emancipation and disciplinary practices have become the warp and weft of the fabric that in social work is known as the 'helping' relation', does not automatically have to lead to the normative view that the life world is being colonised.

By means of the three quality criteria of prudent care discussed above social workers can prevent neo-conservatism from becoming synonymous with rationalisation and professional responsibility from developing into social disciplinary practices.

Literature:

G. van der Laan, Legitimatieproblemen in het maatschappelijkwerk. Utrecht, 1990. Kunneman, H., De waarheidstrechter. (Diss) 1986.

Notes:

1) The Bolderkar affair refers to a scandal involving a Dutch medical day-care centre which pursued a policy that led to the removal of a great number of children from their homes by order of the juvenile court, after allegations of sex abuse by their parents or guardians. An important element of the procedure used to establish whether incest was involved was the 'dolls method' with

which a play situation was created to encourage children to express themselves about sexual advances made at home.

[2]Supervisory Board, 25.11.77.

1.4 Aspects of Qualitative Research

Mark McLean, Research Assistant (Manchester Metropolitan University)

Many of the issues I would like to introduce today have arisen during the course of my research into community-based means of 'dealing' with offenders aged 15 - 21 years in England and Wales, the Netherlands and Germany. In more detail this has involved the comparative examination of policies, practices and definitions of 'punishment' in the community, through review of the available and relevant texts in the respective countries and via semi-structured interviews with those professionals involved with 'community sentences', 'alternatieve sancties' and 'ambulante Maßnahmen'

The purpose of the research is not to identify superiority in any one criminal justice system or exemplify any particular working practice, as van der Laan and Giller (1990) suggest such an undertaking would be 'problematic', and in my opinion fairly pointless and uninformative, as jurisdictions vary in structure, style and development thus making them legally and socially incompatible.

However, it is clear that central issues of concern do exist across 'geographic boundaries' giving the 'translatable concepts' (Heidensohn 1991) necessary for comparative criminological study. In my case interest was focussed upon assumptions and conceptions of justice/freedom, punishment/ education and the experiences of disempowerment or marginalization of individuals relating to aspects such as gender, ethnic origin and immigration.

As such my search for 'new' knowledge became almost instantly entangled in the problem of how to construct a suitable interpretation and analysis of such a wide variety of experience.

Initially I was faced with the issues of subject as object in research and the 'authority' claimed by 'experts' who present findings to 'laymen', a position suitably stated by Mehan: 'I have trouble with this conception of the uses of research for a number of reasons:

1) it treats research as static information, a thing to be transferred between people like a package;
2) it separates researchers from the larger community by treating the community as a passive audience, whose role is to accept the findings of research;
3) the researcher assumes a privileged position vis-a-vis the larger community because of the presumed superiority of knowledge gathered by scientific methods. (Mehan 1979: 204).

From this it can be seen that the research process in association with a particular ideological interpretation can serve to simultaneously expose and disguise, to highlight or hide difference in a complex of competing discourses in which 'words, expressions, propositions, etc., change their meaning according to the positions held by those who use them ..... and from one discourse to another even where there is a supposedly common language' (Pecheux 1975: 111).

So, it was my intention to attempt an alleviation of such problems by promoting a 'continuing dialogue' to provide participants with ways of looking critically at social circumstances, so that they, themselves might take action to effect change or reform.

The appropriateness of appropriation, the authority of knowledge

The significance of critical interpretation rests in the challenge it offers to the conventional constructions of deviance, offenders and the various means of dealing with them which may be found within legal texts, the criminal justice policies of institutions and State apparatus and the pedagogical training of 'professionals'
Many researchers have highlighted the power imbalance or differential which exists between offenders and the State (Foucault 1977, Cohen 1985, Peters 1988), members of the criminal justice system (Mair 1987, Trenczek 1991, van der Laan 1988) and in the contradictions which exist within notions of 'punishment' (Dorner 1991, Spierenburg 1984, Garland 1991) in terms which express opposition or 'violence' within the blind spots of metaphor and the rhetorical strategies of discourse. Expressions such as 'more humane treatment', 'just deserts' or, as a recently much used phrase in England and Wales suggests, that 'the punishment should fit the crime' not the individual, gives rise to the intuitive, essentialist and 'common sense' understandings presented in many texts and by many practitioners and lay people when dealing with the near mythical concept of punishment and the treatment of offenders.
As such I would suggest that the complexity of power relations thus established creates an in-built barrier to critical analysis and change, particularly when such issues as diverting offenders from court or custody arise or when 'traditional' views of dealing with offenders are challenged and questioned.
Further, as a researcher, I feel it is important that the privileged position of the researcher in relation to the researched be subjected to reflexive consideration so as to 'undermine existing conventions of representations' (Felski 1989: 31). In this way the construction and manipulation of such relationships, although challenged frequently within main-stream social science, can be further assessed to avoid the textual 'appropriation' of the researched (Said 1989) and direct attention towards difference and individual subjectivity of experience within a social world.
This position is particularly relevant when dealing with social policy which is often formulated on the macro-social level with the intention that it 'performs' effectively on the micro-social level for individuals and small groups. Here the avoidance of appropriation and the highlighting of difference can serve as a methodological device for a researcher to achieve a positive 'empowerment' for participants in any research.

The term 'appropriation', whilst literally meaning 'to take possession of', has been conceptualised by Said (1989) to further emphasise the basis of power in social relations. By indicating the position of colonised and coloniser hesuggests a means by which the experiences of the colonised may be 'located in zones of dependency and peripherality' (Said 1989 : 207) which are subsequently used by the possessors of more 'dominant' discourse to establish or maintain a particular representation or concept of 'the other' within an ideological position.
This analysis may be applied in research where the characteristic features of the dominant relationships of coloniser/colonised can be identified. In my case not only in the obvious situation of law enforcer/law breaker but throughout all levels of the criminal justice 'hierarchy', such as prosecutor/judge, social worker/client, offender/victim; in the broader relationships of women/men immigrant/citizen, black/white; and also in the relationship of researcher/ researched.
As such this practice creates a complex, interlocking, self-fulfilling and constraining concept of 'authority' in social relations. From the work of Foucault, Said suggests that through the 'erosion of the classical consensus' language can no longer be regarded as a transparent medium through which truth and reality can be simply apprehended as they are, but as a mediating form of representation that is fully implicated in power relations. Foucault sums up the situation as; 'the positions and viewpoints from which people speak ..... the institutions which prompt people to speak ..... and which store and distribute the things that are said'
(Foucault 1979: 11).

In this way it can be seen that language and texts through continued use by those in 'dominant' positions or through reference by writers designates that discourse as 'authoritative', creating textual authority from which they in turn may benefit.
To expand this point. Said identifies two ways in which textual authority is constituted.
Firstly he indicates 'strategic location' which fixes the location of the author in relation to the material about which she/he writes, and secondly he notes 'strategic formation' to define how texts acquire 'mass, density and referential power among themselves and thereafter in the culture at large' (Said 1978 : 20).
In this way he locates the author by the narrative style adopted, the structure of presentation, the images, themes and motifs employed. In my case the study of legal and social policy texts locates many 'authors' in many situations within institutions and governmental 'apparatuses' (Althusser 1970), where the material content of such texts acquires meanings which only exist in the concrete forms of differing social and institutional practices and not within any general system of language. Hence 'strategic formation' occurs amongst texts and the referential and authoritative 'cycle' proceeds to produce a system of language maintained through the 'mapping of a system of relationships of substitution, paraphrases, synonymies, etc. which operate between linguistic elements - "signifies" - in a given discursive formation' (Pecheux 1975 : 112).

However, Said criticises the notion of scholarship as facilitating the development of new knowledge suggesting alternately that the affiliation of each work to others in the field increases its own referential power whilst simultaneously 'disguising' its own modes of representation. From his own work he noted that within the flow of reference and representation the impact of the novel is reduced by a series of comparisons between the new and the familiar. This results in a 'filtering' of the new through the old so that the new is suppressed in favour of the old and potentially destabilising impact of new knowledge is subverted by a process which permits the established view to retain its dominance (Opie 1992).

In this way a perpetual mediation of interpretation occurs to reinforce the hegemony of the authoritative position of certain texts to give a situation in which:

'knowledge no longer requires application to reality; knowledge is what gets passed on, silently, without comment, from one text to another ..... what matters is that ideas are there, to be repeated, echoed and re-echoed uncritically' (Said 1978 • 116) thus progressive contributions to accepted knowledge at first create waves or changes within a field but are quickly absorbed and the discourse mediated so that a new stability or accommodation is reached.

This situation is very apparent when the legal texts of systems which employ codified law are examined. For example the development of the 'Jugendgerichtsgesetz' (Juvenile Penal Code) in Germany from its position in 1923 where it is stated that; 'The penal system is to be used against a juvenile with the intention of promoting his education' (S. 16 abs. 1) was such that the educative content of juvenile punishment was emphasised to the point where 'education was the key' (Pipelow 1989).

Similarly in the reforms suggested during the Weimar Republic the intention was to push back the concept of punishment. It was proposed to extend the youth penal code to include 18 - 21 year olds as well as to increase the 'punishable' age of minors up to at least the sixteenth year and provide a range of educative measures for 14 - 18 year olds which would 'divert' them from the penal code.

However, the intention to create a 'synthesis between criminal law and education' (Hartung 1930 : 54) based upon pedagogic concepts popular in the 1920's was never fully realised, as not only conservatives but many reformers believed that state punishment should not be given up and the reform of the penal code was threatened by stagnation, financial difficulties, frustration and increasing opposition (Dörner 1991).

Yet the 'pressure' of reform was maintained through the strength of the pedagogical discourse which had served the function of 'archaeological episteme' (Foucault 1972), that is a structure of knowledge concerned with a peculiar transformation of behaviour and thought, where reforms of the JGG created a system to empower the 'new' language of education.

Thus the 'zeitgeist' of the 1920's gave rise to the 'tradition' of education within the JGG, or did it? As Foucault would suggest such terms function within a 'history of ideas' to unify disparate elements and synthesise difference. Tradition as a levelling agent simplifies the problems of acceptance creating a concept of untroubled transmission from one generation to the other, in this way terms such as 'biologically criminal survived unchallenged until recent revision (Trenczek 1991). Similarly zeitgeist or spirit of the age claims a casual link between phenomena merely on the basis of whatever is contemporary is necessarily related and in this case, as we have noted, opposition to certain pedagogical reforms was present. Finally it is clear that knowledge was passed on and mediated through successive texts as the JGG of 1943 was able to stand "denazified" until 1977 as the basis of youth criminal law (Cornel 1984).

This 'process' is not uncommon, certain parts of the Criminal Justice Act of 1991, the most recent legislation for England and Wales, still requires consultation with the Children and Young Persons Act of 1933 to fully outline the Law.

As such Said's outline of the process of generating and transmitting knowledge is applicable across many fields, including the practice of social science research, and indicates the potential for appropriation and the 'smoothing' of difference which may occur through the researchers 'ideological' position. Thus if one adapts the 'strategic form' within an area of research it is necessary also to change the 'strategic location' of the researcher.

Empowerment and inner reform

The crux of the argument presented is that to develop 'new' knowledge in an established area it is necessary to change the accepted textual practices in that area, especially those practices which maintain a colonising or appropriative relationship between the participants, along with the researcher/ researched 'syndrome' This is particularly relevant in my situation where I am examining those 'normal and comfortable' structures, institutions and discourses which comprise the greater part of our everyday lives, law/morality, justice/freedom, individual/society. In this way deconstruction, best defined in my opinion as 'a positive technique for making trouble' (Norris 1991: 2), represents the required link between 'crisis' and 'criticism' where any shift in radical action must always entail a shift in interpretive thought.

In line with this position Opie (1992) identifies the 'solution' to the problem of appropriation and the relationship between the researcher and the participants of research to be in the researchers handling of the texts produced by the research, indicating that a deconstructive textual practice may reduce appropriation on 'several planes' by:

1) an identification of the constraints ideology can impose on data;
2) the indirect empowerment of participants by writing texts which represent a range of positionings within the field under investigation;
3) a discussion of ways in which interpretive control can be shared between researcher and participants.

(Opie 1992: 57)

As such a deconstructive reading presents the opportunity to mediate the problems of authority, 'internal' validity and appropriation but will not totally overcome them, as Foucault states, 'whatever signifies or has meaning can be considered part of discourse. Meanings are embodied in technical processes, in institutions, in patterns of general behaviour, in forms of transmission and diffusion and in pedagogical forms' (Foucault 1977: 200).

In this way it is impossible to escape discursive constraints and the 'suppression' they entail, as it is also impossible to write 'beyond ideology' (Threadgold 1986), yet this does not detract from the 'paradigm' as mitigation of the 'poles' or extremes of positionings can occur, 'a deconstructive reading does not attempt to be definitive' (Opie 1992: 57). It is necessary to be aware of the limitations of text in relation to a 'non-appropriable' stance regarding participants locations, self included. It should also be noted that deconstruction itself is not a method, as Derrida states, such a position would involve a reductive misunderstanding, inevitably to follow the path of structuralism from a powerful protest against discursive assumptions to end as just another method to say things about well worn texts.

Thus to avoid 'centring' it is advisable to continually re-examine the ideological position from which the research is conceived, the particular 'truths' and stereotypes which develop from it and the basis from which questions are posed.

In my case an initial interest in the post-modern, with its often sophisticated and persuasive criticisms of foundationalism and essentialism allowed me to examine the 'meta-narratives' of legal texts and policy documents with deconstructive 'vigour' For example consider the following passage from recent legislation in England and Wales:

> 'The Criminal Justice Act makes significant changes to the structure and range of community sentences, with the aim of promoting community sentences as realistic and demanding punishments in their own right'
> (Guides to the Criminal Justice Act 1991).

Immediately we are confronted with 'structure' suggesting an innate entity in the system along with an hierarchical formation, something we refer to in England and Wales as a tariff or 'sliding scale' of measures to deal with offenders. This concept is deemed not to exist or operate in any way by the judiciary and magistrates who operate within this structure and stands in direct opposition to other parts of the new Law, notably S. 29.

Further the need to promote such sentences as 'realistic' and 'demanding' establishes a violent hierarchy to the effect that both are contaminated by addition of their couplet as 'un-realistic' and un-demanding' thus the logic of the text after substitution would indicate that such sentences were not realistic or demanding.

As such we can see how the fairly obvious intention of the 'writer' to presuppose the nature of such punishments is challenged and in the relationship of difference affects the initial suggestion that 'significant' changes have been made whilst also 'diluting' the position of punishment within the passage.

To-finish the 'writers' logocentric use of the phrase 'in their own right' suggests an entity to punishment and a situation arises where this 'content' exceeds the structure of the sign hence the signifier becomes a replacement for the signified and we are left with the promotion of punishment as idea rather than practice, tapping into the variety of concepts of 'punishment' which have existed through the years.

However, one is always drawn back to the conception of post-modernism in which criticism floats free of any theoretical grounding and as such creates limitations in the premature foreclosing of possibilities for social criticism on a meaningful level for participants. Hence we are left with the disabling weaknesses of post-modernism; political naiveté and androcentrism.

In an effort to counter such problems a re-assessment of my ideological position involved the consideration of feminist techniques of social criticism, which represent more the demands of political practice, through the struggle against sexism and the use of cultural or social theories which aim to identify the constitutive features, disempowerment and oppression. Yet one is still faced with some of the essentialist and a-historical features of meta-narratives, universalisation and lack of difference. Thus a mediation of ideological positioning for the researcher can result in positive benefits for the outcome of the research in terms of recognising the potential limits of a particular 'stance' whilst also addressing problems of appropriation. In my case the use of 'post-modern-feminism' (Fraser and Nicholson 1991) has meant that large historical narratives need not be abandoned whilst complexly constructed concepts of social identity, gender, race, ethnicity can be temporally and culturally 'fixed' allowing a focus upon cross-cultural or trans-epochal dimensions in a comparativist rather than universalising approach.

Returning to the production of text, Briggs (1986) suggests that all data is inherently unstable, yet such instability is rarely recognised in research reports. For myself instability may well arise through the number and selection of participants, being both small (by quantitative standards!) and opportunistic respectively, but the greatest potential for imbalance would appear to be my lack of language skills to the effect that the number of texts available in English varies greatly whilst interviews were conducted in Germany through an interpreter and in the Netherlands in English. So much for coloniser/colonised!

However, Opie (1992) suggests that the writer should introduce difference within a text, creating a report which is more 'fissured', where competing voices within a society can be heard. As such the varied 'localised narratives' (Lyotard 1984) which form the basis of my research can be 'vindicated' against both modern totalizing meta-narrative and true 'scientism' which is generally hostile to such data. Similarly the 'otherness' of participants is seldom fully acknowledged in research reports, as Said states, 'this kind of scrubbed, disinfected interlocutor is a laboratory creation with suppressed, and therefore falsified, connections to the urgent situation of crisis or conflict' (1989 : 210). Thus it is necessary to diminish textual appropriation by the appropriate selection of 'voices' within a text to highlight or indicate the inevitable contradiction, paradox and marginalisation which occur. To achieve this it is suggested by Opie that attention be paid not only to the content of interview but also to their textual features, such as intensity of speaking voice, emotional content or tone and the contradictory moment - the occasion when simultaneous affirmation and negation of an issue occurs, for example:

> 'We do not get many girls on work placements .... the courts treat them the same as boys it's just that they are less criminal .... of course the ones we do have must be found placements for women, in kitchens or hospitals ... the usual ...'

similarly,

> 'Firstly they don't speak the language and have a different cultural background .... they don't know the rules of our society and then they are insecure and act aggressively .... when they come to the project we try to integrate them into the group, but there are some young people who don't like aliens .... it is difficult at the moment ...

Here we can see the attempts to validate one side of a contradiction by the speakers involved, a device which serves the function of reducing the contradiction by offering 'mitigation' rather than addressing the core of the problem, the differential treatment of women and ethnic groups through sexist and racist stereotyping. In this way a deconstructive reading attempts to bring out the logic of the texts language and not the logic of its authors claims as we have seen, a situation which can also empower the research participants:

> 'When I look for a community work placement I consider what the person has to offer ... I am not bound by the rules ... before today I have placed convicted drug addicts in a kindergarten ... they like children and if you speak to them they are children in many ways .... I could get into trouble for this, but not so far ... (shrugs).'

Thus a community service social worker who felt disempowered by the constraints of regulation took a conscious decision to contribute significantly to a social issue prompted, as it later transpired, by a desire to 'help others' which was being achieved at the functional level by making such a placement and also at the level of social criticism by making the experience available to research and posing the counter question, why not place a drug addict in a kindergarten? In this way the marginality of position was addressed by opening an experience to 'public gaze', especially where the subjectivity of individual practice ran against 'official' policy, and the 'in-built' therapeutic aspect of reflexive re-evaluation resulted in empowerment of participants at the personal and political level.

An additional benefit of the 'interactive' process of interviewing is the part played by the interviewee in the interpretation of data, even in my situation where semi-structured interview schedules were employed there was sufficient flexibility to allow 'points of interest' to be pursued and for participants to 'prioritise' their responses to questions, in many cases supplying additional information to highlight points of difference and counter the general consensus that can occur through ac-

cepted discourse or knowledge.
In this way qualitative research may incorporate many 'voices', positionings and interpretations into texts, from the powerful and familiar to the marginal and silenced, it may also address the problems of appropriation and textual authority through adjustments to structural form and location, whilst simultaneously assisting in the empowerment of participants in research. Long live subversion!

References.

Althusser, L. (1970) Ideology and Ideological State Apparatuses. in Lenin and Philosophy. London: New Left Books.

Briggs, C. (1986) Learning How to Ask: A Socio-linguistic Appraisal of the Role of the Interview in Social Research. Cambridge University Press.

Cohen, S. (1985) Visions of Social Control. Oxford: Polity Press.

Cornel, H. (1984) Geschichte des Jugendstrafvollzugs. Ein Plädoyer für seine Abschaffung. Weinheim: Basel.

Dörner, C. (1991) Erziehung durch Strafe - Die Institutionalisierung des Jugendstrafvollzugs zwischen 1923 und 1943. DVJJ - Journal 3/1991-

Felski, R. (1989) Beyond Feminist Aesthetics: Feminist Literature and Social Change. Harvard University Press.

Foucault, M. (1972) The Archaeology of Knowledge. New York: Harvester.

Foucault, M.(1977) Power/Knowledge. New York: Harvester.

Fraser, N. and Nicholson, L. J. (1991) Social Criticism without Philosophy: An Encounter between Feminism and Post-modernism. in Nicholson (ed) Feminism/Post-modernism. Routledge.

Hartung, F. (1930) Die Strafrechtliche Behandlung der Jugendlichen und Minderjährigen. in Hegler, A. (ed) Festgabe für Reinhard von Frank zum 70. Geburtstag. Tübingen.

Heidensohn, F. (1991) Convergence, Diversity and Change. in Heidensohn and Farrell. (eds) Crime in Europe. Routledge.

Home Office (1991) Guides to the Criminal Justice Act. HMSO.

van der Laan, P. and (1991) Giller, H. Comparative Juvenile Justice Systems Analysis; An Anglo-Dutch Initiative.

van der Laan, P. (1988) Innovations in the Dutch Juvenile Justice System. in Junger - Tas and Black (eds) Juvenile Delinquency in the Netherlands. Kugler.

Lyotard, J. F. (1984) The Postmodern Condition: A Report on Knowledge. University of Minesota Press.

Mair, G. (1987) Interpreting Probation Practice with Ethnic Minorities and Women. Home Office Research Bulletin 25.

Mehan, H. (1979) Learning Lessons: Social Organization in the Classroom. Harvard University Press.

Norris, S. (1991) Deconstruction. Routledge.

Opie, A. (1992) Qualitative Research, Appropriation of the 'Other' and Empowerment. Feminist Review.

Pecheux, M. (1975) trans. (1982) Language, Semantics and Ideology: Stating the Obvious. London: MacMillan.

Peters, A. A. G. (1988) Main Currents in Criminal Law Theory. Gouda Quint.

Pipelow, L. (1989) Erziehung als Chiffre. in Walter (ed) Beiträge zur Erziehung im Jugendkriminalrecht. Köln: 1989.

Said, E. (1978) Orientalism. London: Penguin.

Said, E. (1989) Representing the Colonised: Anthropology's Interlocutors. Critical Inquiry. Vol. 15.

Threadgold, T. (1986) Semiotics - ideology language. in Threadgold, Grosz, Kress and Halliday (eds). Language, Semiotics, Ideology. Sydney: Pathfinder.

Trenczek, T. (1991) Das neue Jugendstrafrecht. Neue Justiz Nr. 5, 6 und 7/1991.

1.5 Action Research and Methods-Development in Social Work

H. Oostrik/Centre for Professional Innovation and Methodology Development (C.B.M.)

I. Introduction

What gave rise to the following observations is the problem of so-called "double hermeneutics" in action research. This concept refers to the distinction between interpretations of their actions by those researched and the interpretations by those engaged in the research of those actions. In the research I do with professionals in social work this problem is doubled, because in this case there is in addition the question of the interpretation by the professional of the
actions of his clients. My proposals for a narrative paradigm are meant as a means of conceptualising the coherence between these levels of interpretation and of working with them in research.
By way of introduction I want to make some remarks about the importance of (action) research in aid of methodology development in social work.
This professional field is still characterised by a certain speechlessness. Not so much where professional practice is concerned:(this would seem to depend almost exclusively on speech as its essence), but rather in relation to one's capacity to clarify what it is one is doing when dealing with clients or participants. In this sense there is a chasm between theory and practice, between methodology and methodological action.
In sectors like social work there is a proverbial need of insights and trends of thought that describe the essence of the discipline, marking it off clearly against its competitors. As for example against the caring professions or against psychotherapy. In social work as well as in other social professions we are forced more and more to produce a clear profile and to legitimise ourselves (in the first instance in relation to those who fund our work).
At this stage I do not want to expand any further on the causes. I just mention it as the context within which my research is taking place. The action research I am engaged in aims at throwing light on what it is professionals in social work are doing, and the qualities they manifest in their work.

In the methodical action of social workers I distinguish four areas:
1. The programming: the development of work or assistance plans
2. The methodical staging: the presentation to the clients of the various work forms.
3. Active listening in assistential dialogue.
4. Creating a climate conducive to giving assistance.

In what follows I will pay particular attention to no 3: active listening in dialogue. I do so because in my opinion this aspect of methodical action, while being essential to it, suffers most from remaining invisible.

2. Practice feelings, practice narrative, practice theory.

When starting out as a researcher to try to make visible the qualities of social workers, and to put into words the methodical content of their action, one will have to take for granted that the social worker himself already possesses the knowledge necessary to act methodically.

Action research sets out from the acceptance of competent actors, in this case the existence of methodical skills which have been learned through socialisation within the practice of social work. These skills, this knowing-how-to-act (methodically) coincides with the action itself. It is evident from it, it is shown in a mastery of skill or art of, e.g. assistance.

In the words of Argyris and Schön [1] one could call this a form of "silent knowledge", because it is shown, but need not necessarily be expressed in words, Boutdieu in this connection [2] speaks of 'le sens pratique', of a feeling based on practice, which occurs to the actor as a form of intuition forming the basis for his improvisations.

This practice-based feeling, this skill, is developed in formation processes, often subconscious or half-conscious, which form the socialisation process within a particular practice. And in as far as it happens consciously we speak of practising and learning in practice.

Though in the practice of daily life many skills are not put into words, remaining something taken for granted, this is not the case, or at any rate less so, where the action of professionals in Social work is concerned. On the contrary, in this field a practice has developed of translating methodical practice feelings into practice narratives. Just think of work discussions, in which case discussions occur more or less systematically.

Using a term of Lyotard [3] one could speak here of narrative knowledge. This narrative knowledge does not coincide with the silent knowledge of the skills (although this tendency does indeed exist, but more about this later), but is rather a first way of putting into words what is shown in action, in skills, in practice feeling. In that sense it is a construction, an interpretive elaboration.

The narrative constructs the action as a 'matter of course'. It relates how events or actions have taken place, what happened to a person. In short, it follows the course of events. A narrative is composed of the answers to a series of questions: "and then?", "and then"?, which gives the narrative its characteristic rhythm. It translates action into words as a narrative action. In that action a particular action model, a plot may become visible. In any case it shows how people deal with events and what impact these events have on them. In this way the narrative makes attitudes visible. One is either victim or hero, clever or stupid, virtuous or immoral, empathic or businesslike.

Often practice narratives are also in a figurative sense a 'matter of course'. By which I mean that they show a realistic attitude. They tacitly presume that, in contrast to what happens in literary fiction, what is being narrated renders reality the way it is. It creates the illusion that the narrative coincides with reality, like the practice feeling does with the action, as a result of which it is self-evident. When for example one reads reports by social workers of their conversations with clients, the impression is often created of a factual narrative. It is precisely this extensive description of the facts that strengthens the realistic illusion of the narrative.

The 'true story' has a certain impact on both the narrators and the listeners. It locks them inside the narrative, inside this particular version of reality, and by doing so it excludes other versions. The true narrative is the dominant narrative !

Narrative knowledge will evolve only, and more narratives and versions will be told only if one succeeds in breaking through this closed character, which is characteristic of many practice narratives.

Development of narrative knowledge takes place through guess-work. It is a form of knowledge comparable to that of the classic hunter who squats down to examine a broken twig or another detail in the landscape. The broken twig is a trace enabling the hunter to tell: "Somebody passed this way'. The story in a nutshell!

Similarly the opening up of true practice narratives will have as its aim to look for traces in those narratives which will make it possible to hint at other versions of reality, or other narratives. This knowledge through guess-work is precisely the knowledge aimed at in social work.

There still is a third form of knowledge. Besides practice feeling and practice narrative we know practice theory.

Practice theory, too, is a construction of action skill. It describes this skill as a set of rules and as the right way of following these rules. In practice theory action is rule-guided action. The rule has an 'if..then', 'if X..then Y' form. Or in the way Argyris and Schön write in their definition of action theory: "in situation S (the behavioral world), if you intend consequence C (the governing variable), do A (action strategy), given assumptions a...a".[4]

To construct action as rule-guided action means to design it as purposeful behaviour. In the words of de Groot [5]: from purpose as thought towards effect as determined, where he presupposes that the two do not necessarily coincide, so one should avoid the error of reducing action exclusively to one of either: to the formulation of purpose or the determination of effects. In action theory the rule is not so much a precept, as in a rule of etiquette, but rather a constitutive rule, as Searle[6] calls it. A rule as in a game, which enables us to manifest ourselves as practised chess players or skaters. And since we are using the metaphor of chess, we could use it in addition to clarify the difference between conventional and strategic rules. Namely the difference between the rules of the game (with a knight you can only jump and with a bishop you have to move diagonally) which have been fixed on the basis of convention, and the moves one can make with the help of these rules. It is precisely in this strategy: in the moves he actually makes, that the player shows himself a master. In social work methodology approaches the form of a practice

theory. It somehow resembles a manual which indicates how one can make one's moves, a repertoire of methodical rules, which enables us to act strategically.
Practice-theoretical knowledge is developed by explanation. This can be done previously by explaining action, for example in terms of a plan entailing a logical sequence of steps directed towards a determined aim. In other words by designing action. But it can also be done afterwards by explaining how a certain behaviour is the effect of preceding action.
In their book "Theory in Practice", Argyris and Schön distinguish two forms of practice theory. namely 'theory in use' and 'espoused theory'. In the light of the foregoing considerations I would like to paraphrase this distinction in order to place the various kinds of practice knowledge into a certain context.

The scheme looks as follows:

theory in use	practice feeling or silent knowledge	(shows capacity to act)
theory in use / Espoused theory	practise narrative or narrative knowledge	(puts into words a narrative action and shows an attitude)
Espoused theory	practice theory or theoretical knowledge	(describes an action systematics)

Action research aims at the development of practice theory. Its purpose is the reconstruction of action skills in rules, that is to say, in our case, in the explanation of methodical action and in the designing of methods, which in their turn can be practised.
In a certain sense action research is always narrative because, apart from observing practice, it will make special use of practice narratives for its theoretical reconstruction. Action research is narrative in as far as it establishes a dialogue between practice narratives and practice theory. In the case of action research into the methodical action of professionals, which precisely and especially uses narrative knowledge in order to support people in improving their action, interaction between practice feeling and practice narrative will be the subject of research.
Consequently this research should develop a practice theory, in which the interaction between practice feeling and practice narrative, between 'showing' and 'telling', is described as a strategic field.

3. The counselling dialogue as a practical demonstration of narrative interpretations.

The problem of double hermeneutics in relation to the methodical action of social workers, in dialogue with their clients, can be translated into a practice theory on the interaction between the showing of practice feeling and the telling of practice narratives (showing and telling).
In order to succeed in formulating such a theory we will have to bear in mind that we are dealing with three kinds of action: a. the action of a single client or a group of clients; this action can be aimed at improving a situation, but not necessarily so. At any rate it gives cause for requesting support, thus giving rise to a second level of action: b. the dialogue between social worker and client; and finally c. the dialogue between researcher and social workers.
These action fields or practices differ from one another, but at the same time they are involved with each other in a specific manner. We could describe them as levels or layers in the narrative process and the interaction between these levels has a narrative character.In the dialogue between worker and client the action of a client is framed. The social worker does not deal directly with the (problematic) behaviour of the client. It is a question of 'reported action'. The client talks about it in the counselling dialogue. As a result the social worker does indeed deal directly with the narrative action of the clients.
That action is shown, while the action in the daily life situation of a client is framed in the counselling dialogue with a social worker. And in its turn the methodical action of the worker can be framed as a narrative action in a research dialogue.
The counselling dialogue, the framework within which narratives are told and commented on so that the participants in the dialogue may learn from it, also manifests itself as a narrative. The learning process is staged as a journey. We start on our way together and wander around in the narratives that are being told till the exact moment when the 'penny drops': that moment when the narratives take a turn, allowing other versions of the narrated reality/to emerge. From the point of view of the research we are therefore always dealing with a narrative within a narrative within a narrative. The narrative of the clients within the narrative of the social worker about his methodical action within the narrative of the research.

This could be schematised as follows:

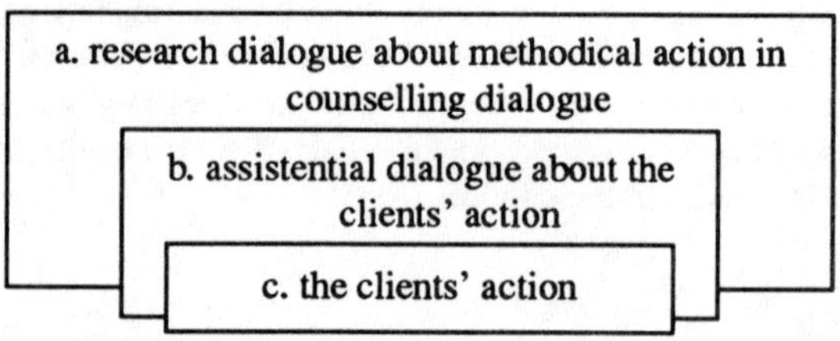

This framing of narratives within narratives produces an effect of Chinese boxes. In a movement which in principle is endless, reality disappears into a box full of images and double layers.
In narratology one speaks of a mirror text. The secondary narrative famed within the primary narrative refers to the first narrative. The secondary narrative has a function in the primary one. [7]
In earlier publications on this subject I have used, in order to clarify this, the metaphor of the frame narrative. "k refers to a literary genre, in which various short stories are told which are framed within the frame narrative. Thus Sheherazade tells her fairy tales in a Thousand-and-one nights in order to escape from certain death. In the Decamerone of Boccaccio various storytellers have gathered in the mountains outside Florence trying to escape from the outbreak of plague in the city. The analogy with the literary genre could even be extended to the meaning of frame narratives. Time and time again the frame narrative is characterised by the motif of 'salvation'. By telling stories one manages to survive.
Something similar could be said of the educational conversation, in which narratives (often in contrast with day-to-day storytelling) are also told in order to escape from predicaments (ambivalences, contradictions)". [8]
The counselling dialogue can be seen metaphorically as a narrative in which the partners 'set off on their journey' in order to learn from the narratives told in this framework.
Or conversely, the narratives are told in an counselling dialogue with a didactic motive. Partners in the dialogue are looking for 'learning moments' in the narratives. The dialogue makes it possible to step aside and as it were confront the narrative. The dialogue as a frame narrative is a sum-total of asides, of comments, that are made by the way, in the passing by (or of) the narratives.
Consequently the aside is the form of the interaction between frame narrative and secondary narrative. True enough it interrupts such a narrative, but it does not stop the telling of the story. In secondary narratives we look for traces, traces from which we can reconstruct a frame narrative about learning.
As I already indicated above, such double layers in the telling of the narrative signifies breaking through the illusion of reality in the telling of the story, as a result of which an 'as if comparison, a play with the reality of action becomes possible.
Within the framework of the educative dialogue telling the narrative can then result in demonstration. The realistic attitude vis-a-vis reality is disturbed, so that also other attitudes can be demonstrated. In the demonstration showing and telling are joined. By hinting at other versions of reality the narrative dialogue becomes a practical demonstration of narrative interpretations.
In order to elucidate the concept 'practical demonstration' I want to make use of the genre of the 'problem narrative'.
Like all practice narratives also the problem narrative is a narrative construction of the action skills implied in a problematic practice. In the narrative the speaker shows how he is dealing with the problems, which attitude he is taking up in rela-

tion to them. This he does from a certain perspective, usually his own, through which events take a certain course.
This narrative construction is also a social construction.
By this is meant that this form of lending meaning has a function in the practice to which it refers. Narratives not only say something about a practice, they also affect it in some way. Normally speaking practice narratives are conservative. They back up the practice by presenting themselves as 'a true story'. In other words: the true narrative serves the cause of keeping reality the way it is.
Consequently changing a practice presupposes seeing through the construction character of narratives and the telling and living of other narrative options, other narratives with respect to a particular practice.
The specific characteristic of problem narratives is that they not only render a problem, but that the telling of it is itself often part of the problem. In the telling of such narratives there is an effective dialectic of what is being told' and what the telling of it does, in other words the effect it has on the speaker and the listener. And this effect, too, can be part of the problem in hand.
The technique of practical demonstration is a means of dealing with this double effect in a productive way.
Let us look at the narrative of a problem drinker, because it could serve as a standard example for the dialectic just mentioned. In his narratives the problem drinker will present his drinking behaviour as the solution of the problems he is facing.
Now practical demonstration aims at making visible a contradiction (or a similarity) between this narrative and what the narrative does, what it shows (showing and telling). This presupposes that the listener does not allow himself to be sucked into the closed circle of the ordinary narrative, which is told as if self-evident. But it does not mean either that such a narrative as that of the alcoholic has to be rejected as untrue. Active listening consists precisely in observing the attitude (of the alcoholic) vis-a-vis reality, as shown in the narrative. The actor shows a version of reality which for him in one way or another is functional. It is obviously or secretly in his interest to tell the narrative in such a way, and to present it as true.
By being aware of this, one creates sufficient room in the dialogue to insinuate that the 'real' problem is that the alcoholic does not really want to tackle the problem. ('real' is put in inverted commas, because this version should not in its turn be presented as the true narrative, but as another narrative interpretation from a different point of interest).
In this way one can explain that such a person presents himself as a victim, (the expression 'it always happens to me' as the standard metaphor for victim), and at the same time hint at his active role (not wanting the problem to stop).
The advantage of this interpretation is that it narratively constructs the problem situation in a different manner.
The course of events is reversed. Instead of saying that there are problems and that therefore one takes to the bottle, this version suggests that it is the drinking that causes the problems.

In the dialogue with the drinker one can demonstrate this interpretation on the basis of his behaviour.
The technique of the social worker comes down to a practical demonstration of narrative interpretations [9]. Practical demonstration means that one shows as it were the interpretation, the other version of reality. The fact that a narrative is told within the framework of a dialogue makes it possible to move to and fro between what one hears in the narrative and what one sees in the narrator. Just as an interpretation of a painting can be made only really clearly if one stands in from of it and can point directly at it, so the narrative interpretation, which the narrative is, can be made clear by pointing to the attitudes of the narrator, to what he shows.

4. Research

Our research presupposes that the practical demonstration of narrative interpretations in dialogue with clients is a diagnostic method typical of social work, A diagnostic which is not made about the client, but which emerges in dialogue with him. The purpose of research is to describe this narrative diagnostic from the perspective of the professional, namely as rhetorical elaborations and interventions of the social worker in the narrative process. In this way our research alms at composing a catalogue of intervention designs, or more accurately, of narrative dialogue strategies.
This research makes use of case studies. In extensive interviews social workers talk about their action in assistential dialogues on the basis of concrete cases. These interviews are analogous with the elaborations applied by the these social workers themselves in dialogues with their own clients. You could call them narrative interviews [10].
Subsequently the research takes a further step. The reports of the interviews are analysed (together with the participants in the research) with the help of a set of guiding concepts which has been developed on the basis of previous investigation. This analysis takes place as a form of consensus investigation. Proposals about identifying and naming various dialogue strategies are submitted in successive rounds to the panel of the research group, until a certain consensus arises.
Apart from those concepts resulting from consensus investigation, concepts for a guiding framework are also taken from classical rhetoric (in particular the 5 key concepts from the ‘tractatio’ or treatment of the subject-matter: inventio, dispositio, elocutio, memoria and pronunciatio) [11]

Dialogue strategies or commentaries are subdivided in three chapters:

(1) The inventio or the finding of the narratives(or imagination) This includes:
a. Stimulating the narrative (a.o.by addressing the clients as narrators and by creating a narrative atmosphere)
b. Selecting themes (a.o. by further questioning on events: what happened, who

were involved, how did they turn out etc.)

(2) The elocutio or the practical demonstration of narrative interpretations (or: imagination and contradiction). One interrupts the narrative process by:

a. Contradicting what has been narrated, that is to say noticing details until then meaningless (e.g, in the manner of telling the narrative) or omissions (in the narrative), and contrasting them with what is being told (in the trio: to observe something, to note this, and to associate on it)

b. Creating 'as-if'situations, in other words creating room for other versions of reality by changing the perspective of the narrative (one proposes to try to visualise the situation from the perspective of another person), or through metaphorical language (one brings sleeping metaphors to life or introduces a new one).

(3) The memoria or the repetition of new interpretations(or exercise) Here one can think of:

a. The development of commonplaces (for example through the repetition of a characteristic quotation, the introduction of a central metaphor or the designing of a scheme).

b. The theorising (for example by way of the explanation of social contexts and behaviour patterns).

The rhetorical systematic I am developing puts special emphasis on a description and categorisation of the different forms of comment on narratives by the social worker. Consequently what matters most to me is the identification and categorisation of action strategies, and not so much the description of the various 'guiding variables'. I am more interested in the what-question, the how-question and the when-question than in the why-question.

I mention this in passing, in order to indicate a difference with a great deal of methodical action theory, which stresses aims and then goes on to systematise action as in a phased plan.

Action research with professionals in social work shows a certain analogy with social work itself, in as far as it elaborates, jointly with those participating in the research, their narratives and know-how. Just like in social work the idea is to learn in the face-to-face relation of oral use of the language. One sees and hears the narrators 'act' and one listens to the narratives about their action. And one works with them on the spot through the practical demonstration of narrative interpretations.

In research, too, the same thing happens, but in principle research takes a further step. It is looking for a practice theory. And a theoretical analysis is only really possible by taking down the narratives (on video and in writing).

Narratives and the context of the narratives are analysed as a text. Such a theoretical analysis leads to abstraction, to a conceptual summary, an action systematics. (Although this can be experienced as a help by social workers, more often it is felt by them to be an impoverishment compared to the riches of the narratives and action itself).

Starting from the above-mentioned 'narrative within the narrative' model, the action researcher makes two contrastive movements. First a movement from inside to outside, resulting in a practice theory. And a movement from outside to inside, in which the theory in the 'as if frame of narrative knowledge can be used and tried out in methodological action.

Notes:

(The numbers in the notes refer to the bibliography)

[1] Cf. 1.

[2] Cf. 3., especially p.77

[3] Cf. 6., especially p.67 ff.

[4] Cf. 1., p.19

[5] Cf. 5., especially p.69

[6] Cf. 10., especially p.33 ff.

[7] Cf. a.o.2.,p. 143/144

[8] Cf. 8., p. 12

[9] I have taken the concept of 'practical demonstration' from Michael Baxandall, as elaborated by Renee van de Vail in an article on the work of Barnett Newman (Krisis 46.1992. p. 15).

[10] Cf. 11

[11] Cf. Lausberg, Heinrich, Elemente der literarischen Rhetorik. München 1982., p.24 ff.

Bibliography

1. Argyris, Chris and Schön, Donald A., Theory in practice. Increasing professional effectiveness. San Francisco/London 1976.
2. Bal, Mieke, Theorie van vertellen en verhalen. Inleiding in de narratologie. Muiderberg 1980.
3. Bourdieu, Pierre, Argumenten. Voor een reflexieve maatschappijwetenschap. Amsterdam 1992.
4. Giesecke, Hermann, Pädagogik als Beruf. Grundformen pädagogischen Handelns. München 1987.
5. De Groot, A.D., Begrip van evalueren. 's Gravenhage 1986.
6. Lyotard, Jean-Francois, Her postmoderne weten. Kampen 1987.
7. Oostrik, Hans, Aan het verhaal ontsnappen. Narratieve gespreksstrategiëen in de agogische conversatie, in: TVA 1991 (I), p. 32-44.
8. Oostrik, Hans, Narratieve agogiek. Aanzetten tot een kritisch agogische methodologie, in: Praktische Humanistiek (1/4) 1992, p. 5- I 9.
9. Oostrik, Hans, Narratieve gespreksstrategiëen. Een narratieve benadering van methodisch handelen in vormingswerkgesprekken. Interne uitgave. Nijmegen 1992
10. Searle, John R., Speech acts. An essay in the philosophy of language. London/New York 1970.
11. Schütze, Fr., Das narrative Interview. Zwischenbericht an die DFG. Bielefeld und San Francisco 1979.
12. Tannen, Deborah, Talking voices. Repitition, dialogue, and imagery in conversational discourse. Cambridge/New York 1989.

1.6 Doing Research by Using 'Official' Data

David Boulton, The Manchester Metropolitan University, England

This paper explores the usefulness of official dam for comparative research on both a national and an international basis. It explores the limits imposed on the researcher's ability to create and answer questions by prior decisions about what information is collected. It raises the question as to whether international co-operation on the design of schedules for the collection of official dam is desirable and possible.

Introduction

The extent to which researchers can use 'official data' in order to explore areas of interest will depend on the extent to which officials and researchers view the social world in a similar way. It seems clear, at the outset, that officials and researchers are frequently likely to have different perspectives. For example a question in the Census (1991), carried out every ten years in England and Wales, asks each household to indicate the number of rooms which are available to the household. The information which results from this question is used, amongst others., by local authorities, carrying out the statutory obligation to provide housing, to measure whether, or not, a family is living in overcrowded conditions. The definition of 'overcrowding' which is used in this exercise is often a crude measure of :people per room'. What counts as a room will have an effect on this measure, and, therefore, the reasoning which lies behind whether a kitchen counts as a room is interesting. If a kitchen is "less than 2 metres, or 6 feet 6 inches wide", (two measures which are not exactly the same) then it is not counted as a room; if it is at least that wide it does count as a room. Research into such important social policy issues as inadequate housing provision has to wrestle with such problems, and these problems are often difficult to avoid where official data is all that is available.
Here, as in a multitude Of other aspects of the everyday lives of ordinary people which are recorded by officials, researchers have no control over the form of such data. Although people are what has happened to them - officially they are what Officials decide they are. Such officials decide, from all that has happened, what is important to know. When asked informally who they are, people are free to select from all that has happened and even from what they wish to be. When officials ask people who they are, officials control what is selected.
If we focus on data collection processes in official contexts it becomes clear that the resulting data reflects the thinking of an individual, or group of individuals, at a point in time, about what is seen by them as important. Rarely, if ever, do outside researchers or users of the service have influence on the form in which such data are collected. The Government Statisticians Collective (1979) stated:
"Official statistics are produced primarily to provide the information required by

administrators, 'mandarins' (the very highest civil servants) and ministers in government departments...Academic researchers and other users of published data are, not surprisingly assigned the lowest priority of all in GSS (Government Statistical Service) planning." Cop 146-147).

Not all official data is under the direct influence of such high level officials, although there is little .that is completely untouched by them. The legislative process, however, places requirements on agencies, 'at levels below central government, which Clearly influence their information collection activities.

This lack of control over the form in which official data is collected has important consequences .for all research which is based upon them. When the researcher wants to add a comparative dimension to the research, whether based on within-nation comparisons, or on international comparisons, a new set of problems is presented.

In order to explore these issues a case study based on research into police custody records will be used for illustration. Clearly other examples could be used and it might be worth exploring the extent to which the difficulties which are identified in this case also apply in other areas.

The case study: Police custody records

The Police and Criminal Evidence Act (P.A.C.E) was introduced in England and Wales in 1984. The Act had two broad aims: [1] to give the police sufficient powers to investigate and detect crime and [2] to ensure that the rights of individuals were free from unnecessary interference. Part IV of the Act introduced important changes to the law. It imposed limitations on police detention, created the concept of 'designated police stations', made provision for the appointment of 'custody officers', detailed their duties and prescribed general responsibilities in relation to detained persons. It also created a system for reviewing the detention of persons held in police custody; imposed limitations in respect of persons held without charge, detailed the circumstances under which a person could be detained after charge and dealt with a number of smaller issues .relating to police custody.

In January 1986 the Home Secretary issued 'Codes of Practice' (H.M.S.O. 1986). These were approved by Parliament and were revised with some 200 changes in 1991 in the light of experience and after "extensive public consultation" (H.M.S.O. 1991). As a result of the Act the 43 police forces in England and Wales were required to change the method they used for recording information about prisoners who were taken into custody. Individual Force policy dictated the procedures which were adopted to accompany the Codes of Practice and some of these procedures were designed to ensure that an adequate record was kept.

Thus, although the legislation applied to the whole of England and Wales, its execution in terms of record keeping was carried out as an internal exercise in each of these 43 forces, some extremely small e.g. the City of London Police Force (798 officers in 1992), and some extremely large e.g. the Metropolitan Police Force

(28,509 officers). Some police forces cover largely rural sparsely populated areas e.g Cumbria Police Force, and some like Greater Manchester Police Force cover densely populated urban areas.

The purpose here is not to identify and list differences between forces but rather to point to possibilities of difference which could have an effect on particular policing issues and therefore act as modifiers working against a uniform interpretation and application of a particular piece of national legislation. This will be contrasted with Sweden where there is a national police force and where on all important issues a standardised interpretation is applied regardless of distinctive local or regional differences.

England and Wales: The Custody Record Form.

The Codes of Practice for P.A.C.E. set out the basic ground rule which relates to the custody record:

"A separate custody record must be opened as soon as practicable for each person who is brought to a police station under arrest, or is arrested at the police station having attended there voluntarily. All information which has to be recorded under this code must be recorded, as soon as practicable, in the custody record unless otherwise specified." (H.M.S.O. 1991 p.39).

An examination of the Custody Record sheet in current use in eight of the forty three forces indicates similarities between the information recorded but also reveals many differences of substance. 62 specific items are required on at least one of these forms and only 18 are common to all eight forms. These eighteen are set out in Table 1, as follows:

Table 1. Information Present on Eight Police Custody Records: England & Wales

1. Police Station	2. Reason for arrest	3. Prisoners rights read
4. Notification of a named person	5. Request for solicitor	6. Officer opening record
7. List of personal property	8. Disposal of property	9. Arrested by:
10. Surname	11. First Names	12. Address
13. Occupation	14. Age	15. Date of Birth
16. Height	17. Sex	18. Date & time for all entries

Items 1 to 9 relate to specific requirements of P.A.C.E. With some special exceptions an arrested person must always be taken to a 'designated police station' [1]. Chief officers of police are required to designate police stations for the purpose of detaining arrested persons and for each designated police station 'custody officers' [6] of at least the rank of sergeant, must be appointed.

There is a provision that if a custody officer is not available an officer of any rank can perform the functions of a custody officer. What is important here is that, in order to avoid any conflict of interests, and to ensure impartiality, the arresting officer [9] cannot perform the functions of a custody officer.' All .entries on the custody record must be dated and the time recorded [18].

When a person is brought to a police station under arrest, or is arrested having attended Voluntarily, the custody officer must inform the prisoner of his/her rights [3] i.e the right to have someone informed of his/her arrest [4], the fight to consult privately with a solicitor and the right to consult codes of practice. The arrested person has a number of other fights e.g. the right to information on the grounds for detention, the fight of communication with her/his High Commission Embassy or Consulate, if she/he is a foreign national, and a number of fights to e.g. written notice of entitlements while in custody and arrangements for obtaining legal advice. These are subsumed under [3] in the above list. Items 10 to 17 include personal details of the arrested person which serve identification purposes.

This group of variables could provide the basis for research comparing the data within and between the eight police areas in this sample. For example since the Code of Practice for detention sets out the purpose of this part of the Act as: "All persons in custody must be dealt with expeditiously, and released as soon as the need for detention has ceased to apply". (H.M.S.O. 1991: p 37), it would clearly be possible to treat the time spent in custody as a dependent variable with relevant independent variables included in a model for comparison between forces.

Clearly academic researchers are not the only people interested in such issues. Indeed, since information of this kind is recorded in the context of a piece of national legislation, since the information contained on the custody record is concerned with the rights of individuals, and since such information is potentially important, in a legal context, where it can be used to confirm or disconfirm the proper application of those rights, it will be clear that those who are monitoring public services such as the police are likely to be using the data in their own quality assurance work. For example, although not exploring the detail of time spent in custody, Chief Constables are required to include information in his/her annual report on the number of people kept in police detention for more than 24 hours, and subsequently released without charge, as well as details about warrants of further detention beyond 24 hours.

Thus official data of this kind is not collected with the researcher in mind although monitoring and internal research issues may clearly have a bearing on the way in which they are collected and stored. As soon .as the researcher wishes to step outside the boundaries of the local area problems of incompatibility of data are likely to arise. Even in situations, as here, where the local area is constrained by national legislation, differences in the data recording process are likely to reduce the range of variables available for comparison and are likely to make some comparisons difficult or impossible.

For example only three of the eight custody record forms examined here specifically request information about the 'ethnic group' of the detainee. A comparison

between police areas of whether members of different ethnic groups are treated differently in the custody process is, therefore, impossible; or at best can only be done on a limited basis. That such 'ethnic monitoring' is important, to ensure anti-discriminatory practices, is self-evident, but it can only be carried out in those areas which have included the request for information on the custody record.
In terms of comparisons of ethnicity, even between these three police areas, a further level of difficulty arises. The coding for 'ethnicity' is operated differently in these three areas. One form leaves a space for an open-ended answer following the information name 'ethnic origin', and although at this time there is guidance available to the custody officer as to the categories to be used, practice before 1991 left the construction of categories to the custody officer. A second force requires information for 'ethnic appearance' and offers six codes: 1. White European, 2. Dark European, 3. Afro-Caribbean, 4. Asian, 5. Oriental and 6. Arab.
It is worth noting that 'ethnic appearance' and 'ethnic origin' are not the same concept and it may be that custody officers would operate these concepts differently. The third force does not offer a concept for the variable, rather it offers four boxes-for ticking which are separately labelled as Black, Asian, White and Other. It is noticeable here that any Comparative work on this issue would have problems relating to the matching of values as well as the previously mentioned problem of conceptual similarity.
A further dimension of difficulty arises here. In order to make proportionate comparisons between the general population and those for whom a custody record has been opened the obvious source for comparative data would be the Census, in which the categories for 'ethnic group' are once again different i.e. White, Black-Caribbean, Black-African, Black-Other, Indian, Pakistani, Bangladeshi, Chinese, Other. Here, 'ethnic group' is defined in terms of descent and the possibility that a person could be "descended from more than one ethnic group or racial group" is taken on board by asking the respondent to "tick the group to which he/she considers he/she belongs" (Census 1991).

Thus any research which aims to compare the custody records of police forces in England and Wales is faced with a number of methodological problems for which there is no obvious solution other than 'doing the best you can'. These can be identified as:

[1] Problems relating to comparing different points in time which result from changes in the process of recording information,

[2] Problems relating to comparing different places which result from the relative autonomy of police forces in designing the record form,

[a] where legislation requires the inclusion of a category these problems are likely to be minimised but not eliminated, and

[b] where there is no legislative-requirement these problems will be maximised,

[3] Problems which result from interpretations made by the custody officer, or others completing the form, which reflect individual differences,

[4] Problems relating to the storage of information and its effects on retrieval of data which have been previously recorded.

In relation to this last point, it is worth noting that only one of the eight police forces represented here stores the custody record information on computer at this time. In each of the other seven cases the information is recorded on paper and is stored as paper. This has three important consequences: [1] Custody records for those who are not arrested for serious crimes are not kept indefinitely and will be destroyed, making comparisons over a relatively long time period impossible; [2] the place where the data is stored will have an effect on the ease of retrieval and [3] retrieving this type of data will always be a slow and laborious task.

Custody Records: Sweden

'In Sweden there is a national police force and many of the forms which are associated with police work are therefore standardised. Even under these circumstances there are locally produced forms, for example for making observations on a person held in custody.

Three main forms are used to record information about a person who has been arrested. These forms can be cross-referenced through a number. Firstly there is a form which records personal details (Personblad). Information recorded includes all items which are shared by the forms for England and Wales with the exception of Height and Age and Date of Birth. These latter two are unnecessary because all Swedish residents have an identity number which includes date of birth as well as a code which indicates whether a person was born in Sweden or not. Additional information which is missing from the forms for England and Wales includes Marital Status, Place of Registration (of birth or residency), Workplace Address and Telephone Number, and whether a driving licence is held. Other information which is shared by some of the British forms includes Previous Surname, Alias, Telephone Number, Place of Birth and Nationality. These similarities and differences are summarised in Table 2:

Table 2. Custody Records: Personal Details Recorded.

	England & Wales		Sweden
	All Forces	Some Forces	
Person number			Yes
Surname			Yes
Previous Surname	Yes	Yes	Yes
Date of name change			Yes
Alias		Yes	Yes
First Names	Yes		Yes
Marital Status			Yes
Address	Yes		Yes
Telephone		Yes	Yes
Occupation	Yes		Yes
Workplace address			Yes
Workplace telephone			Yes
Age	Yes		
Date of Birth	Yes		Indirectly
Place opf Birth		Yes	Yes
Height	Yes		
Sex	Yes		Yes
Ethnicity		Yes	
Nationality		Yes	Yes
Driving License held			Yes

The Second form (Arrestantblad) repeats some of the personal information and includes details of arrest and detention as well as details of transfer or release. Interestingly some quarter of the space on the form is devoted to recording details of intoxication including the smell of the breath which has to be described in some detail, the method of intoxication and details of confiscated alcoholic drink. Only two of the British forms formally require some of this information; both use three point scales: sober/had drink/drunk and appeared sober/slightly affected by alcohol/drunk although details of drunkenness would be likely to be recorded in the open observations section which is a part of all the British forms.

The third Swedish form (Omhändertagandeblad) is concerned, in considerable detail with the social and medical care of the prisoner.

Research, therefore, which aims to compare custody records within Sweden is not affected by a lack of standardisation of the data collected and, to some extent, is unaffected by problems associated with access, since much of the essential information is stored on computer,. There remain problems relating to the comparison of different points in time which are a result of changes in the process of recording information and problems which result from individual interpretations made by custody officers, and others involved in the process of completing forms.

Thus the extent to which comparative research is possible within a nation seems to depend on the degree of central, regional, or local control of police forces. Comparisons are clearly possible in Sweden, whereas in England and Wales the relative autonomy of individual police forces makes such tasks difficult.

This simple comparison of the police forces of two nations points firmly to the conclusion that comparative research between nations will be characterised by a similar, if not greater, degree of difficulty to that experienced in England and Wales. The relative autonomy of nations in organising the recording of official data will ensure that these difficulties remain in the foreseeable future:

The question raised for comparative research is whether co-operative attempts should be made to explore possibilities for standardising the recording of official information. In the case presented here there are points of similarity which could provide a starting point for such attempts. Clearly this issue stretches far beyond police custody records to include all situations where records relating to service delivery are kept.

Changing the frame of reference

Having established that, at the present time, comparative national and international research using officially collected statistics is plagued by problems of definition, selection of variables etc. a question remains as to whether the data which exists could be used, in other ways, as a basis for comparative work. Cicourel and Kitsuse (1963) suggest a basis for an avenue which could prove more fruitful than the approach set out above:

"...these difficulties arise as a consequence of the failure to distinguish between the social conduct which produces a unit of behaviour (the behaviour producing processes) and the organisational activity which produces a unit in the rate of (deviant) behaviour (the rate producing processes)." (p. 132).

Cicourel and Kitsuse were concerned with theoretical and methodological difficulties which had arisen in the study of deviance, such that different approaches had failed to achieve theoretical integration. The problem presented in this paper is a different one. It has been argued that integrated analysis of officially recorded data is frustrated by methodological problems associated with the recording of behaviour.

If the emphasis is shifted to comparative research on the rate producing processes, the disparity between recording systems, which was earlier identified as an obstacle becomes the focus for the research. For example the apparent focus on alcohol and intoxication in the Swedish forms may be seen as evidence to support a claim that, for those who designed and approved the forms, alcohol appears to be impor-

tant in the processes of police work, social work and criminal justice. At the comparative level, the relatively low profile of prestructured categories for intoxication and alcohol available in the British forms would suggest a lower priority. An exploration of what is pre-coded on forms, as against becoming a possible entry under an 'open-for-comment' section, may provide evidence of what is considered to be essential information in the process which the form represents. An 'open-for comment' section is included in all the forms examined here and is used to record full details of any action or occurrence involving the prisoner including full particulars of all visitors and visits by police officers; i.e. there is a requirement for written comments to be recorded about events as they happen during the custody period. One interesting development of the use of this section of the form was noted in the case of the one British police force which has recently computerised its custody record procedures. Unless specifically deleted by the keyboard operator, entries relating to the co-operative demeanour of the detainee, compliance with the Codes of Practice and the absence of complaints, medical conditions, marks or injuries, are automatically printed in the 'open-for-comment' section. It seems possible that on the next occasion this form is redesigned these topics may . well become part of the pre-coded part of the form.
It is argued, therefore, that a comparative examination of the rate producing processes would be useful, and achievable, and would provide evidence for an examination of the everyday concerns of members of an organisation, or at least of the perceptions of those issues which are considered important by the people who designed the forms. discussions With such people, and perhaps,. as importantly, With those who 'operate' both the forms and the service could then provide useful tests of the validity of conclusions which are reached on the evidence of the forms alone.

List of references:

Census (1991) H form for Private Households, London, H.M.S.O.

Government Statisticians' Collective (1979) How Official Statistics are Produced: Views from the Inside, in Hammersley M. (ed.) (1993) Social Research: Philosophy, Politics and Practice, London, Sage.

H.M.S.O. (1986) Police and Criminal Evidence Act 1984 (s.66): Codes of Practice, London H.M.S .0.

H.M.S.O. (1991) Police and Criminal Evidence Act 1984 (s.66); Codes of Practice, London, H.M.S.O.

Kitsuse J.I. & Cicourel A.V. (1963), A Note on the Use of Official Statistics, Social Problems 11.

2. Internationale Perspektiven der Sozialen Arbeit und der Ausbildung von SozialarbeiterInnen

2.1 The Effect of British Policy and Ideological Imperatives on Promoting European Links in Social Work and Education

Malcolm Payne

Introduction: Recent developments in British approaches to European social work

The British attitude to mainland Europe and its inhabitants is that of the islander who wants the safety of a dividing stretch of water, but is prepared to navigate across if there is any advantage to themselves. This is a stereotype, of course, but Malcolm Hill (1991, p 15) has recently characterised the British view of social work and the European Community as 'approaching with caution'. He suggests that Britain has three main orientations to other countries:

- to the Commonwealth, a loose grouping of former colonies, for historical and political reasons
- to the USA for reasons of shared culture and language and some shared political interest, and
- to Europe, because of close proximity and the consequent political involvement.

The first two orientations are declining. The Commonwealth nations have their major links and political allegiances within their own geographical and political spheres, and the historical link grows weaker; there are few advantages to be gained from a link with Britain. The USA, with the ending of the east-west 'cold war' conflicts, is loosening its ties with and interests in Europe, and may come to see it as a competing economic entity. Also, Britain's 'special relationship' with the USA based on historical links and alliances and shared language comes to seem less important because of Britain's declining economic and military power, and increasing power within Europe evidently being focused on Germany and a closer alliance of central European countries. Since Britain's ambivalence about closer relationships with Europe has led to some uncertainty about the extent of its influence in this inner grouping, outside countries such as the USA and Japan look to links where the power is, rather than where there are relatively minor cultural and language advantages.

In social work, the same historical process is taking place. Much British social work has been fundamentally American; the major American texts have been used in Britain for teaching social work, and there is an interchange of literature with the American literature having the greater influence. As former colonists, British social work, drawing on the American, has had some influence on the development of services in many African and Asian countries, and has gained a perspective on community development which has affected its approach to community work, through the writing of people such as Batten (1962, 1967).

Of Europe, and of social work within it, British social workers have little knowledge, and they have few contacts. The shared cultural perspective and language which allows British social work to use the American literature restricts the understanding of and priority given to European social work. There have been some moves in this direction over the past few years, stimulated by closer British involvement in the European Community and its funding and regulatory mechanisms. This has led the major body in British social work education, the Central Council for Education and Training in Social Work (CCETSW), to follow a policy of financing and supporting activity in international matters only in Europe. The result of ERASMUS and similar schemes has led to greater exchange and contact between British and other European higher education institutions.

This experience in the 1980s gives us enough experience to make some judgements about how British policy on links with Europe in social work education is working and some of the difficulties and obstructions. Three points are evident, and form the basis of the argument in this paper:

- the traditional wariness and lack of contact between Britain and mainland Europe leads to substantial managerial and financial obstructions in promoting contact between social work in Britain and mainland Europe
- the cultural links with the USA has led to the importation of a perspective on 'anti-discriminatory work' which has gained an overarching priority in social work development in the UK during the late 1980s and early 1990s, and this has distracted attention from trying to overcome the practical and managerial difficulties in the development of contacts with social work in Europe, and
- as a consequence, the historical links with Commonwealth countries which have led to the existence of significant ethnic minority communities from Africa, Asia and the Caribbean in Britain has prompted a continuing focus on Commonwealth contacts which also reduces the priority given to European contacts.

I deal with each of these points in turn. My *aim* in this paper is to propose that in working on international links, we tend to think of the practical problems of the particular projects that we are involved with. I want to suggest that two things lie behind these. In the first place, our concern with the immediate practical problems sometimes blinds us to the importance of more general problems such as the nature of our students, staff and the issues which face them in their daily work. An ERASMUS grant, a European Community grant to encourage student mobility, is of little use, for example, if the type of students for whom we provide have limited opportunities to travel because of their family responsibilities. The second point is that these problems are in turn conditioned by policy and ideological aims within our social service and educational systems and personnel, which we need to identify and respond to.

If this proposal has some value, I suggest that colleagues in different higher education systems and institutions need to examine their own practical, policy and ideological issues, and I offer this paper as an example of some of the points which might be found in one particular system.

Managing obstructions in Euro-relationships

Managing relationships between British social work and related courses (which for convenience I call 'community studies' courses) raise particular problems and issues which are unique within higher education, although there are parallels in many cases in other disciplines and other disciplines also have their special problems which we forget in our involvement in our own issues.

A number of 'community studies' problems arise which are to do with students

- they are not the average sort of students who come to higher education with examination successes at the age of 18; this means that they have to be discovered and encouraged to apply to come, and they have to be found experience and academic qualifications which will allow them to gain admission to higher education
- higher education in the UK is selective, and the convention is to select on examination success; if one does not select on examination success, what criteria does one use, and how does one ensure that selection is fair?
- before people are allowed to enter professional courses in community studies they must gain experience of life and experience of the services in which they work; the course needs that rich experience to base its work on, particularly as, in European terms, British courses are relatively short, so that students must learn quickly, accept considerable personal stress and be able to bring experience and academic competence to bear in their courses fairly quickly
- because students are not straight from school, which is the conventional pattern in British higher education, they have many family pressures on them, which 'ordinary' students do not suffer; "they are more likely to be married, to have children, to have elderly parents to care for, to have family and financial commitments and all this puts an extra strain on them, which because it is organised to cope with 18-year-olds without family responsibilities, our higher education institutions find it difficult to help with
- having been unsuccessful in their early educational career, many of our students are under-confident, or legitimately anxious about their ability to cope
- having been out of school for some time, many students are not accustomed to the adult learning approaches and flexible learning that characterises our approach to education, and expect formal teaching and learning; they may be pleased that this is not what they get: on the other hand they may be concerned by the lack of structure
- like most people in Britain, students are not taught European languages, there is a shortage of language teachers in schools and elsewhere, and their allegiance to and interest in Europe, rather than the Commonwealth countries from which many of heir ancestors came is variable; so government and other pressures to-

wards greater integration with Europe do not inspire some students

- travel is relatively expensive from our northerly island, whereas students from the European may have much easier opportunities to travel more cheaply overland and thus better opportunities to learn more about other countries, languages etc.
- because of a professional wish to have proportions of the black population in the country reflected in the proportions of workers in the field, we are taking a high proportion of black students, many of whom have suffered educational disadvantage due to racist oppression in their history, and this also involves extra help
- they suffer particular problems from the financial stress of undertaking placements, with expenses paid in

There are also problems for the management of staff presented by the sort of work we do

- British higher education is financed on a basis which encourages the admission of more and more students for less and less money, and the personal help and small classes which have always been assumed to be necessary for practical community courses are harder to finance
- placements in agencies occupy between 40 and 50% of the courses, these have to be organised, assessed and supported; this is not required by a conventional academic course
- staff must maintain their experience in the field, as well as teaching, administration and research which is the duty of all teachers in higher education, yet practice experience is not highly rated in terms of promotion and regard in higher education
- staff are relatively expensive, because they have to have experience in the social services first before coming to their academic post; so they come in at a relatively senior level; the cost of older experienced staff cannot be balanced by younger (and cheaper) staff
- problems of the integration of theory and practice are big issues for academics in our field, in a way which is often completely ignored by more academic courses
- professional bodies set special requirements for the courses we provide which are more onerous and expensive than for the average degree course, but which are not accounted for in the financing of courses
- new requirements imposed on all courses for involvement in learning about information technology and computing, and for European connections, requiring language learning, must be added to the practical and learning demands of our courses, which are already too short for their professional contents.

No doubt other examples of these problems might be cited. This, however, is enough to give the flavour of the particular combination of problems that community studies face. First, students are likely to have more personal difficulties inconnection with their course, they are likely to have had a more varied and difficult pathway to their professional education and may need to make up much more from a background of educational disadvantage. They may find it difficult to get access to higher education at all. There are particular difficulties when we consider opportunities for experience in Europe.

Second, the professional requirements for our courses and the work involved is not well recognised in higher education, and resources for our students do not keep pace with their needs.

The consequences of these problems raise particular issues for attempts to share work with students in other countries

- British community studies students have personal and institutional pressures which make it difficult for them to take up opportunities for study abroad
- British education does not provide the resources in language learning to support work in Europe
- Professional courses are pressurised and demanding thus making it difficult to provide for extra involvement in European teaching, and
- making arrangement for European teaching and exchanges is an additional burden for staff which is not well-recognised in promotion and respect in the institution, on top of practice placement arrangements which are similarly weakly recognised.

European money, and in particular ERASMUS and similar mobility schemes, has encouraged some developments in this field, but the declining availability of these funds coupled with greater demands for them, together with the assumption that they will initiate activities which will be taken forward by ordinary funding may mean that future developments will slow. In the UK, government funding for higher education, and pressures on student finance for students who have family responsibilities, mean that in the community studies field may have little chance of taking up opportunities for study in Europe.

These problems may well be exacerbated by the position of CCETSW. British social work education is controlled by a derailed set of guidelines on curriculum and teaching, enforced by a system of validation of courses, annual inspections and controlled appointment of external assessors to each course, who must be appointed from an approved list of people, and produce reports to an approved format each year. CCETSW also issues guidance about particular aspects of courses. One piece of guidance currently being considered concerns arrangements for teaching and especially placements in countries other than the UK.

CCETSW's approach is fundamentally to control courses by setting procedures which include 'checks and balances' on compliance with its requirements. In the case of placements, this includes approving agencies as suitable to provide practice teaching on placements, and training and accrediting individual social workers as practice teachers. In a few years time, it is hoped that no placements will be arranged anywhere without such approval.

Recent draft guidance on placements abroad, issued for consultation, presents the conflict between CCETSW's practice within the UK and the conventions of European shared courses and exchanges. CCETSW considers requiring the home (UK) course to approve individual practice teachers and agencies in the other country in accordance with its criteria, which might well be inappropriate for that country. Of course, this allows CCETSW to maintain its standards and conventions. But it is onerous for both parties, and flies against the convention in most European exchange programmes, including ERASMUS, that mutual recognition of the standards and approach in the country in which the work is being done.

These practical difficulties suggest that stronger policies and efforts will be required to continue British involvement in European relationships in the community studies field. However, there are pressures which make it seem possible that the commitment to developing Euro-involvement will be limited.

Anti-discriminatory work

The dominant theoretical and ideological debate in British social work from the mid-1980s onwards has been what has come to be known as 'anti-discriminatory work'. Three originating streams of thought can be identified. One was a growing concern, stimulated by feminist thinking, about the subordinate role of women in social work, an occupational group where women are in the majority both as providers and receivers of services. The second stream of concern was a growing concern about racism in public life and services, disadvantaging people from minority ethnic communities particularly those originating from Commonwealth countries. Concern grew about their isolation and alienation following a number of inner-city riots during the early 1980s. The third stream of issues derived from concern about people with disabilities and efforts to make public services and social attitudes more responsive to their needs.

Without going into the details of trends in these three areas, an analysis has developed of the issues in each of these areas has been concerned with the way in which the power of established social structures such as patriarchy and cultural dominance is oppressive of 'minority' and relatively powerless groups. Social work has traditionally been at the heart of services for such groups, and there has been a concern to place overcoming such power imbalances at the centre of social work practice. This has led to growing influence for advocacy as an aspect of social work practice and to the growing use of empowerment strategies. The aim is to make social work 'anti-discriminatory' and 'anti-oppressive' in everything that it does.

This approach has not only influenced practice ideas about how social workers might go about their tasks, but sees social work as an important factor in overcoming oppression and discrimination in other services which social workers help their clients to deal with. There has inevitably been an effort to include 'anti-discriminatory' practice at the centre of social work education, so that courses themselves do not discriminate in the selection and management of students, but also so that they place anti-discriminatory practice at the centre and teaching and practice learning. Great effort has been invested by CCETSW in formulating regulations which require this of social work courses, and generating learning approaches and resources which will support it.

These developments should not be thought to be wholly theoretical and educational in origin. Since agencies facing clienteles with much more significant minority group memberships, increasing pressure to respond to the needs of disabled peoples and consciousness of the role of women in much of their work have needed and demanding some of this work, and welcome the greater awareness and responsiveness of newly trained workers.

These developments are significant in relation to British social work's responses to Europe, because the issues faced in Britain are to a great extent rather particular to historical trends and political perspectives available in the UK during the 1980s. The ideas have originally been imported from the USA, through British awareness and use of American literature, where these perspectives are also strongly evident in the 1980s. Some such issues also arise in Europe, where there has been concern for racism in the growth of 'new right' nationalist movements which have been strengthened by fears of immigration, particularly from eastern Europe.

However, British problems are somewhat different from those in America and Europe, particularly in the field of race. The most controversial British minority ethnic communities mainly originate from the 'new Commonwealth' countries of Asia, Africa and the Caribbean and many have certain citizenship rights which come from their original colonial status. One political issue has been the continuing attempts to limit those rights. American race problems stem from a large indigenous population originating from Africa, resident for many generations, originally as slaves. There is a later population of immigrants; in recent years of Latin American origins. In Europe, attention has primarily focused on 'migrant workers' who are generally without citizenship rights; most countries have relatively small communities of ethnic minorities from former colonies.

The approach has also been different. In the USA, the approach has been legalistic, with an attempt to enforce rights and appropriate behaviour. This has only been a minor aspect of the British approach; its equal opportunities legislation in the areas of women and race is relatively weak. Moreover, in America, the theoretical and practice approach within social work has been multi-cultural in emphasis, with much literature concerned with language rights and understanding and involving people from new immigrant communities. In Britain, radical social work theory has shifted into feminist and empowerment approaches, following the failure of influence of Marxist radical and community approaches to social work in the 1970s. Multi-culturalism has largely been rejected in favour of the power and oppression analysis. I have tried to show that the crucial theoretical and practice emphasis in British social work in the 1980s, first of all, reflects peculiarly British needs which are not widely shared within Europe, although aspects of British concerns are present in Europe. Secondly, the thrust has been derived from American cultural influence on the UK, rather than reflecting European issues.

Anti-discriminatory work represents an inward-looking, self-involved concern in turn inspired by one of the traditional non-European cultural influences on Britain, the USA and which is not fully shared in Europe. Its importance for British social work presents a major difference in perspective which adds to the practical and managerial difficulties, discussed above, of promoting an orientation to European concerns in British social work. This becomes evident when we turn to examine the other British orientation outside Europe - to Commonwealth countries.

Links with the Commonwealth

Again, British courses face a conflict here, particularly pressed upon them by the desire to build up anti-discriminatory work. While funding has been available to promote links with Europe, many universities have worked at developing these, and a good deal of expertise has been butt up. Moreover, government policy has been to limit funding through CCETSW to European links, and two curriculum conferences have been organised by CCETSW, and a series of CCETSW publications (Into Europe) have been promoted. At least two texts, considering and arguing for involvement in European social work (Hill, 1991; Cannan, et al, 1992) have recently appeared. However, as an example of be tensions that exist for British social work courses, the international policy of the Joint University Council - Social Work Education Committee may be quoted. This is one of the most important representative bodies of social work professional training courses.
Here is its statement of geographical priorities:

- to give particular priority to contacts within the following geographical areas
- first priority: 'new Commonwealth' countries. This is first priority because links are as yet not well established, but would meet the priority for working with countries and cultures which are under-represented within the knowledge base and organisations of social work. 'Student understanding', 'research' and 'academic and service links' objectives all combine and very little co-operation and development currently exists, as far as we are aware. The aim here should be to facilitate all three of JUC-SWEC's main roles: representation, developing new links and information sharing.
- second priority: Europe. This comes second because there are many good links, and newcomers can rely on the experience available from JUC-SWEC members. The priority for working with countries and cultures which are under-represented is less strong, except in the East. Access through European programmes is currently strong although lessening because of financial constraints on European programmes and inevitably a greater burden will fall upon institutions to finance activities. However, travelling is cheaper, because most destinations are short-haul, and so are more easily financed. We put this above other possibilities, because of the extent of interest in Europe and the need to develop links with the extended EC and the East. The aim here should primarily be our role of information sharing.
- third priority: USA and English-speaking commonwealth. This is included be-

cause we have traditional links and shared traditions, but we put this as lower priority because they do not meet the priority for working with under-represented cultures and countries, and because these countries are relatively accessible because of shared language. The aim here, again, is primarily information-sharing, but the ease of access to the literature of and information from these countries suggests that they should be a lower priority than Europe.'

This statement, because of the needs of anti-discriminatory work clearly places Europe in a lower priority category, and argues strongly for a restricted role in relation to Europe. The third priority, covering the traditional cultural links with the USA and English-speaking Commonwealth, reflects, again, the anti-discriminatory policy but also acknowledges that links here come as third in the priority list because of the strength of existing links and access.

Conclusion

I have sought to show in this paper the conflicting priorities which British social work education faces in building links with Europe particularly deriving from the importance given to anti-discriminatory work and the consequent focus on links with countries with significant minority ethnic communities in Britain. This interacts with the practical problems which British higher education faces in organising links with Europe, so that policy and priorities for British social work do not support efforts to overcome practical and management difficulties. Stronger policy and practical support for links with Europe will be needed to maintain and develop contacts in the future.

Moreover, in a more general way, this paper seeks to argue the importance of careful analysis of the interaction of practical and managerial issues with real policy imperatives if we are to understand how to develop links between countries effectively.

References

Batten, T R (1962) Training for Community development: a critical study of method London, Oxford University Press

Batten, T R (1967) The Non-Directive Approach in Group and Community Work London, Oxford University Press

Cannan, Crescy, Berry, Lynne, and Lyons, Karen (1992) Social Work and Europe London, Macmillan

Hill, Malcolm (1991) 'Approaching with caution: social work and the European Community from a British perspective' In M Hill (ed) Social Work and the European Community: the social policy and practice contexts London, Jessica Kingsley

Malcolm Payne, Professor of Applied Community Studies The Manchester Metropolitan University Department of Applied Community Studies 799 Wilmslow Road, Didsbury, Manchester M20 8RR, telephone: 061-247 2097

2.2 European Certificate for Elderly People

Ton Dales

1. Introduction

In processes of international co-operation concrete results are expected at an early stage.
In other words facts and figures, joint activities, etc. Understandable and rightly so, particularly for financiers and managers in the institute. At the same time the demand merely for this type of results, is one-sided. Another aspect of this co-operation is consequently overlooked completely or dealt with to easily. This aspect is the co-operational process itself. To negate or minimise this aspect of the process, for example by considering this (implicitly) merely to be a condition, that is fulfilled 'naturally', is unjust. For this aspect not only largely determines the 'concrete' results and vice versa. It also has a relatively independent character and a value of its own. Besides, the co-operational process is not at all a natural-one. On the contrary, the guidance, the organisation of a task-directed group and a task-directed process require much attention, great care and knowledge.
In connection with our educational goal, social agogic* education and to some extent also with our profession, this contribution to the discussion is about international co-operation as a process of a task-directed group.
Especially for the coherence of process and product and the supervisional and supporting aspects of this process. The description and the research of this process and the product takes place on the basis of a project aimed at concrete results that we have been working on since 1991: the development of a European Course: 'Social work with the elderly".
So as not to disrupt the course of this story too much, the contents of this project is described in broad outline in an addendum. Our advice is to read this first.

2. Communication

During the first joint meeting in 1991 there was not one common language. We generally spoke German, but sometimes French and Spanish. No-one spoke all of these languages, two was nice, there were also people that spoke only one language. The Spanish delegation depended entirely on a German-speaking colleague. Although there was a large variety of languages, there was also much confusion and delay during the meeting. Afterwards English was chosen as the official language. This was not without irony, because at the time there were no participants from the UK in the project yet. Later still, after further discussion it became apparent that this choice was the right one, as far as the exchange of papers was concerned, but not for the discussions during meetings. True, the French delegation was re-inforced with a member that speaks (some) English.
The Spanish delegation has benefited from their English lessons. But still the

knowledge of English is (at this moment) too little to avail ourselves exclusively of it. At the 4th meeting in 1993, besides English, we shall consequently (as a result of the decision) also speak German, as well as French and Spanish.

* there is no English equivalent. It is a social science dealing with processes of planned change by professionals in the fields of education and social and cultural work.

The language problems introduced by way of this anecdote, are too well-known. However this example demonstrates slightly more than was already known and refers to other problems than communication alone.

1. Due to the fact that projects in the area of internationalisation are usually created by arbitrary circumstances, individual interest or personal hobbies of teachers, but rarely as a consequence of institutional policy, the right people do not always end up in the right place. The fight people need not necessarily be the ones with an excellent control of foreign languages.
2. For as long as and in as far as institutional policy is not yet developed afterwards,
   and support takes place in connection with this (among others in the area of language skills), internationalisation projects will remain personal hobbies of individual teachers. Reversely, they often lack the inclination and ability to transform the project into an institutional policy, although they would be the proper persons to do so.
3. A proper (possibility of) communication is fundamental for more specific processes in task-directed work like information and decision making. Incomplete or false information, misconceptions, which are also, because of faulty communication in the language, difficult to verify and correct, delay and impede decision making.
4. The decision to use one language (English) as official language means making a choice from two possibilities from different starting points. The starting point that focusses on the product, with the expectation that through quicker and more efficient communication (meetings), (possibly more) results will be achieved sooner. The starting point of the operational process of a group, where the issue is the opportunity for each participant to make his contribution, so that a firm task-directed group is formed as a basis for more solid decision making and a better product. This is not just about the production of the one project that is currently worked on, but about acquiring capacities for international co-operation by the participants, the effects of which may be transferred to other projects.
   Neither choice can be absolute. It is a matter of finding the right balance.Obviously this was disturbed by making the demand to speak only English at the meeting (too soon).
   In the concrete situation this demand was weakened, that is to say the person in the chair speaks English, but every member has the actual possibility to (also)

use his own language. Consequently, translations take place regularly during meetings.

It is our experience that short or long breaks are very useful, not regularly but frequently. These breaks can be used not only for translations, but also to discuss and evaluate the items that were discussed in the meeting, to try to work out the proposals, either with members of your own delegation or from another one. Consequently the breaks are very effective and functional in the given situation.

Besides the language there are other factors that make communications extra difficult in a project of internationalisation. The most important ones are briefly indicated, without further elaboration. The geographical distance between participants and consequently the frequency of meetings, the various national cultures and the difference between countries, especially in the fields of higher education, educational institutions and the situation of older people and social work with the elderly. Due to the distance between the participants and the accordingly high cost Of meetings it is not possible to meet frequently. In our experience the 3-day meetings every six months are 'both essential as well as the most that can be achieved.
It is dangerous to bring up cultural differences of an alleged nationally or geographically determined character, because of the nature of this concept in itself and its connotations. Especially because this involves the danger of (hopefully benignant) stereotyping. It was however fairly obvious that there are differences in culture. In this respect it is important not to deny certain matters, without giving in to prejudice, but on the contrary to give them a workable basis.

3. Information

While preparing for a more specific contents of the educational programmes in connection with the number of hours that was determined, the Dutch delegation thought it might be a good idea to define the number of hours as the student workload. This means that the total number of hours available for the programme for the student includes all forms of study: attending lessons, self-instruction, examinations, etc. It is a unity that already functions within the Hogeschool and that has the advantage of uniformity. In a paper that was sent to all members, this concept was introduced and explained. When the issue of the hours came up later in a meeting we naturally assumed that the discussion would be held on the basis of the above definition. However nothing was further from the truth. Obviously the information did not yield the desired effect.

This example also illustrates several things.

1. Needless to say that information is crucial. Especially about educational content, educational organisation and the educational institutions. A clear picture of this situation with all participants regarding all others, with a clear determination of mutual differences and similarities, is partly responsible for the re-

quired mutual understanding and with it for the decision making and in the end for the product. This is all the more important because with the first participation in an international project there is little or no initial knowledge of these matters, so that everyone starts from scratch. Complicating in a project of internationalisation such as ours, the product of which is specialisation of the vocational education, is the fact that similar information about the professional field that is trained for is just as essential.

2. It is easy to overlook the exchange of information as a (relatively) independent element of the work-process, in the supposition that the necessary information will come up while working, or at the time it is needed or required for business reasons. This attitude is partly fight and information that was acquired in such a way may be very effective.
   It is also tempting to provide little or no room for information in the meetings, based on priority and time. Nevertheless there is the risk of a too instrumental use of the exchange and provision of information. This applies particularly to information of a more general nature like for instance the international context on a social, economical, political and cultural level.
   True, this information may be very important, because the education and the work with the elderly is embedded in it, but knowledge and insight in these 'areas can not be linked up directly with the project. It may thus come as no surprise that information about such matters is not structurally discussed in meetings.
   Informally, at table or over drinks, 'off duty', this is the case (occasionally).
   Here also, like in the story about communication the object is to find the middle way in structuring the processes of information: on the one side the information that is more or less self-contained and of a more general 'nature, on the other hand there is the information directly connected with and essential to the solution of a specific actual problem or a certain decision in the progress of the working. process.
   Giving information, and particularly assimilating it into a discussion that functioned in both the aspects that were mentioned at the same time, started out very well initially, in the discussion about method and methodical work with older people. Structuring this was done by three, fairly general questions in aid of drawing up the methodology programme. Participants made a paper as a basis for discussion.

4. The group process

Six colleges of higher vocational education participate in this project. Consequently approximately thirteen people attend the meetings. Most delegations have two or three members. In connection with the language problems, coupled with the intensity of the work-process, this number is definitely the minimum for an internation-

al project. This group of participants is very stable. Since the start two people have left the group and four have joined, one of whom was already known to the participants. In view of the fact that usually (four times already) the same people come together, the meetings, that take several days, are very intensive and considering that also the very scarce spare time is spent together, we may speak of face to face relationships and consequently of group forming.
Next to the business relations, also personal relations, 'likes and dislikes' have developed. Relations that also manifest themselves occasionally, in both respects, beyond meetings and the direct objective of the project as well. Among other things this can be expressed in small personal attentions, private information here and there and the joy of seeing one another again. Undoubtedly a very close group is a condition for a fairly ambitious project such as ours.
After all, the goal of the project can only be achieved on a medium term. On the one hand this requires a lot of tensile force, while on the other hand it involves much and hard work. The risk of (partial) failure can not be excluded beforehand. In that case more than the concrete project is lost. On a limited scale it means a set-back in the attempt for internationalisation.
From this point of view it is important not only to give the process of group forming adequate space, but also to influence it actively. In addition to the task-functions, attention will also have to be paid to climate-functions. In other words: the issue is team building.
This requires a lot of attention for the functioning of the group, especially the culture of the group, group-standards, for mutual (working) relations in the group and the businesslike functioning of individual group-members. There is a wide range of points of attention, like motivation, tolerance, showing everybody's contribution to full advantage, (personal) encouragement and support. But, if necessary also correction, clarification, mediation.
On .these points the group offers plenty of functioning capacities, divided differently among the members. Again, a major handicap when functioning in aid of the group process, is the language. Also the focus on the product constitutes a constant threat for the provision of said contributions.

5. The intergroup

Complicating is also that not only have the participants in the project formed a group gradually, but that at the same time there is an intergroup situation. This implies that every participant is (also) a representative of an organisation, his/her own education. However this does not mean that each participant is also formally a representative or delegate of his/her own organisation. Nor that everyone as such, has equal authorities. This does not depend merely on the organisation of his/her own education and possibly the partial organisation (such as project organisation) that was created by the home-fronts for the benefit of the project.
Especially the mandate of the participants, if and when there is one, is important.

Also important is the formal position of the participant within his/her own education. With the exception of two managers, all participants in the project are teachers. There is no detailed information about possible differences within these teacher positions, for example on the basis of functional differentiations or main tasks. The fact, that all the programme-directors of the institutes that will be participating in the ICP that was applied for, will attend the meetings, almost goes without saying and is positive, but it hardly says something about the authorities that were discussed earlier.
So far information about the position of the participants as representatives of their own school has not been dealt with systematically, but informally it has gradually been acquired. Now that the preparations with regard to content of the course (the development of the curriculum) are in an advanced stage, the time has probably come for actual clarity on this point.
In the concept of this paragraph two remarks that were made earlier, should be mentioned. Particularly for the knowledge of the (representative) position of the participants and in order to understand this, information about the organisation of each education and the educational organisation is an important condition. Secondly this will illustrate the possible disadvantages of the phenomenon that internationalisation projects are often started as a result of the interest and input of enthusiastic teachers or as a result of arbitrary circumstances and are consequently not or not adequately rooted in the organisation and policy of the institute. The impression is that with none of the participants the organisation of the project is clearly rooted in their own organisation.
It is important to look at the project from the angle of the intergroup situation because, as is well-known, the relationship between representative and. rank and file is not or hardly suited to be influenced by members of the group. Even in the sense that in actual fact no influence is possible on the composition of the groups in as far as the individual members are concerned. This also applies for possible formalised positions within the project group, like in our case the chairman, as long as and in as far as they have not specifically been sanctioned by the management of the participating institutions, in which case they act on their behalf. The chairman of the project group is not in this position.
The intergroup situation also means that differences in interest and power between institutions, presented by the participants as representatives, should be taken into account. Of course these differences are also present in the group situation between individual members.

6. Formalisation

The difference in position between participants in the project in relation to their own organisation is merely one factor that has lead to the wish to formalise the co-operation further than is the case in an ICP. The option of rounding a society is the most obvious one to provide a better institutional basis for co-operation. Apart from

this a corporate body may be useful in fund-raising, to cover costs that are not subsidised by ERASMUS. Also the continuance of the project after the ICP will benefit from a corporate body. On a long-term basis this will provide a better basis for innovating perspectives.
On the other hand, rounding a society, considered as a partial-project in itself, will mean more work in the initial stage. Not in the least with regard to the acquisition of the necessary consent from the institutes, because this is not always certain beforehand.
Still, before there is any form of a society, we have given it a name: PRIAMUS. Already the name of PRIAMUS has a significant existence as the name and identity of the project.

7. Decision-making

For the process of working in a task-directed group, especially one of an international level, it is essential not to take the decision making too formally, and certainly not formalistically. This means that it is just as important, and sometimes more important, that all participants can 'witness' and can carry the decision that was taken.
This is particularly important in view of the mutual corresponding problems of communication and information that were referred to earlier, as well as the positions and interests in the project groups that differ in more ways than one. In our situation decisions are not made just about major and important matters with a direct impact on the elements of the programme, the curriculum and the CO-operational arrangement in itself, and are evident as such. Also less obvious items are involved in decision making, often to the smallest, most insignificant detail. Often this is adequately done in the form of the explicit determination of (apparent) concurrence or arrangements that were made. Under the circumstances decision making requires more than the usual care, great accuracy. Decisions are more than the expression of a joint agreement with regard to content, more also than a possible formal definition.
In a formal sense the necessary decision making is expressed in consensus. Materially this means that compromises will have to be developed frequently, to prevent people opting out, as long as this is not absolutely necessary. So far we have managed to do so. As a consequence decision making takes place slowly but surely and sometimes on a minimal basis. Therefore it was decided that during the initial stage (temporarily) the theoretical programme can be taken in the students' own country. Should this have been consistent with the terms of the ICP, a minimum period of only four weeks would have been set as start of a practical period. Another example is the decision for a phased start of the programme with regard to the institute and the programme elements. The starting point is always the (minimal) possibility of one or more institutions.
A practical consequence is also that decision making is used very flexibly. This

means that some times (for a part) we will have to go back on decisions that were made, as shown by the example of the official language. That a decision that was made, is emphatically confirmed or taken for a second time (again), this of course after sometimes lengthy discussion. Reversely, this may lead to a situation in which, sometimes after elaborate discussion, the decision making is postponed. It is therefore possible, that an item is later accepted silently and as a matter of course. This seems to be the case in the issue of student workload that was discussed earlier. Consequently decision making is a cyclic rather than a linear process.
In that sense, besides coherence, there is also an analogy with the process of acquiring and processing information. In this respect we must point out the importance of a good secretariat in general and of good minutes in particular. As a rule it is not possible for every individual education to provide this, since taking minutes requires special skills and involves extra, relatively high costs. Since it is hardly possible to find the solution for these problems within the concept of an ICP, a different form of formalisation, like a foundation may bring the solution. By the way, under certain conditions PRIAMUS may appeal to a pair of very capable ladies that take minutes, who also made the report of the last two meetings.

8. Conclusion

While working on the development of the European Course 'social work with the elderly' we have come across all kinds of processes that are normal for any project. This was proved by describing (parts of) these processes and looking into them superficially.
Evidently the international dimension of the co-operation complicates these processes considerably. Because there is no or hardly any formal leadership in the project, although there is a chairman, there is a greater need for leadership functions practised by members in the meaning that group work gives to this concept. One could say a strong, informal leadership. This requires special capacities and effort from the participants in the atmosphere of attitude, skills and knowledge. Knowledge not only in the area of (inter) group processes and agogic action in general. Also business-like knowledge with regard to content in the area of the task to be performed.
In that sense it is possible to refer to working in projects like this, and especially to supervising them, as a professional task.

1. Objective of the project

The international project named PRIAMUS functions since June 1991 (the date of the first meeting). Its objective is the development of a European course for 'social work with the elderly'.

2. Participants

Participants in the project are:

* Den Sociale Højskole Esbjerg, Denmark
* Institut de Formation et de Recherche en Action Social (IFRAS), Nancy, France
* Fachhochschule (Fachbereich Sozialwesen) Potsdam, Germany
* Fachhochschule (Fachbereich Sozialwesen) Bielefeld, Germany
* Hogeschool van Amsterdam, the Netherlands
* Escuela Universitaria de Trabajo Social 'San Vincente de Paulo', Zaragoza, Spain

3. Programme of the European Course

The course consists of the following subjects:

1. a theory programme 180 hrs
   * living conditions of elderly people in Europe (90 hrs)
   * social politics (60 hrs)
   * health cate and ageing (30 hrs)
2. a methodology programme 60 hrs
3. a practice programme with two forms: 400 hrs
   A. practice with direct contact with clients
   B. research practice
4. an anual intensive programme 40 hrs
5. a colloqium/conference every two years as part of the intensive programme

4. Organization and implementation of the Course

* Subjects 1 and 2 are implemented as initial or as initial and post-initial train ing programmes.
* The common concept of subjects 1,2 and 3 is formed, besides the number of hours, by the shared and specific objectives.
* Credits and certificates will be issued for the programmes
* In the initial stage subjects 1 and 2 can be taken in the student's own country. The third subject requires a minimum period of three months to be spent abroad.
* Before starting with subject 3 a substantial part of subjects 1 and 2 should be completed.
* In order to participate in subjects 1, 2 and 3B, the student should be proficient in the English language. To participate in subject 3A. the student should master the relative language, possibly the language of the clients.
* Subjects 1,2 and 3 can have a phased start per subject and per education. In this a distinction can be made between receiving foreign students and 'sending out'

students abroad. The average start within this differentiation will be in September/October 1994.

* The subjects 3 and 4 are prepared together. By rotation one of the participants in the project will act as host. With subject 4 (and less so with 3) the main responsibility lies with the host as organiser.
* The combined implementation of subjects 3 and 4 took place in 1991 and will be repeated in 1993. In 1993 the implementation of subject 3 was cancelled.

5. The organisation of the project

So far there have been four meetings in aid of project organisation, about twice a year. During' the periods in-between, the participants prepare for meetings by doing homework. In October 1992 a application was made to 'Erasmus', for the recognition of the project as an inter-university co-operation programme (ICP). Preparations for the foundation of a society (study) have started. A chairman has been appointed.

2.3 Boys between Bravado and Timidity

Description of the Dutch project WORKING WITH BOYS

Lauk Woltring

I. Origin and current situation

In 1986 the initiative was taken to develop a project on working with boys at both a conceptual (1) and a methodological level. The first reason were problems in various fields of social work, youth work and education in particular in working with boys.
A second reason were the reactions from professional workers as well as from young, male clients of social work with respect to the emergence in recent years of working with girls.
Classical male working-class-behaviour is riot longer embedded in a strong - be it patriarchical - male culture. The traditional masculine world of work and power is no longer inaccessible for women. Male behaviour that reflects this old world is obsolete. Women's liberation is not a topic of main interest for many young men, and if they do react, it is mainly in a defensive manner, sometimes even aggressively. They often seem to have no other way of reacting to reassignment of roles and sex stereotyping: withdrawing or behaving in a way which is considered to be negative. Changes in the relations between men and women are facts, we should seek the advantages for men as well. "Girls ahead, boys must step back" is not a good message, it does not work. The image of manliness presented to young men however is often a caricature of reality. Many young men cannot, or do not wish to comply with this image.

The interest for gender-specific work with boys is growing in the Netherlands, both from the field of ambulant and residential youthwork and from other fields of youth work as well as general youth policy and the field of education.

In December 1988 the preliminary stage of the current project was concluded with the publication of the book 'Boys between bravado and timidity' (2) and a big conference in Amsterdam with about 600 participants. Central topics since 1990 are:

* male socialisation and male survival and coping strategies,
* (prevention of) sexual violence by, and against young men; redistribution of paid and unpaid work (between men and women, young and old, white and coloured people); and
* working with boys on selfcare and their caring-competence
* working with coloured young men.

In May 1993 a new book emerging from the project will be presented, produced under commission of NIZW, 'Nederlands Instituut voor Zorg en Welzijn' (the Dutch

Institute for Care and Welfare), which is a semi-state body for work development in the entire field of social work, youth work and education. (3)
Since 1989 there has been shown an interest in the WWB project in other countries in the European Community, and outside Europe as well. Therefore this English text.
The project was financed until 1992 by grants and from then on by the return of lectures, consultancy, advice, trainings and developed products.

II. Basic orientation and social relevances

In many aspects young men and women are the same. Yet there are also differences. Besides physical differences there are also differences in the expectations which boys and girls experience in their upbringing, in opportunities for gender-identification, and in their anticipation of social perspectives. As a result of this, boys often develop other skills than girls. It goes without saying that the problems boys encounter are in many ways different from those of girls, the same goes for the qualities they develop to cope with their existence.

I n the classic male upbringing many young men - raised by women and not in close contact with masculinity in their early childhood - are not adequately prepared for their future role anymore, the same goes even stronger for one-parent-families (mostly mother-child families). Girls and women increasingly enter the labour market, also in technical professions, although the access of women to the Dutch labour market has stayed behind in comparison with other developed countries. More and more women want to share the upbringing of children and caring tasks with their male partners. This is a fact that young men have to meet when they enter the market of courting and seek a partner.
However, many boys and men are not prepared for these changes, many of them still cling to a male identity defined in full time paid work (4) and career - even if women can perform the same. Their identity is direct at stake, especially for those were there is no place for on the labour market, when the demands placed upon them are too high, when they have lost their sense of direction, when they can't give importance to their strives and can't give direction to their energy. They cannot go back to having a child - like women can - and can easily fall in despair, acting it out aggressively or turn inwards, escape in taking drugs, finding their way in the competing networks of crime or street gangs. Others are - or feel - impeded in their attempts to fill in their role in a different way.

Boys often do not fully realise their own potential qualities and the possibilities in broadening their options. The focus of attention however is often on boys due to the trouble they cause, their misconduct or the power they exercise over girls. Frequently boys are represented in a negative way in youth work and in the public opinion as a result of their behaviour, often regarded as threatening. Figures from studies on youths in the Netherlands, but also in other countries such as the US and England, continually show the differences in percentage with boys and girls, no matter whether it concerns risk-behaviour on the street, small crimes, drug abuse or violence and sexual offences. It seems to be self-evident, and the resultant reactions by adults in symmetrical escalation sometimes only reinforce this picture, without acknowledging the fact that this behaviour to a large extent reflects young men's attempts to comply with their inheritance. Bravado, sturdiness and dare-devilry often camouflage their insecurity and timidity. Those boys that do not fit in this picture, but turn more inwards get no attention at all, feeling sometimes even ashamed not to match the image of 'real men'.

Every new generation of young men is at their birth saddled with an inheritance of an age-long division of work and power between men and women. This division partially based upon biological & genetic differences is continued by different socialisation: boys are in general raised with too early and too much emphasis on exploring and autonomy before they have established a thorough feeling of attachment and safety.

These experiences in early childhood go together with the lack of opportunities for 'skinclose' male identification and have great influence in the dynamics of later developments in male adolescence. Once they realise that they are male (3 - 4 years old, phase of individuation and separation) they see that their mother is not like themselves. But what is a man? Distant views in the outside world, a father at long emotional distance and caricatures in the media fill the gap. In each other's company boys often play as if they know. Young boys, children still, call each other childish. Childhood is not a positive thing in the conscience of young men. On the one hand: they bluff themselves into masculinity always afraid for the one that sees him through), on the other hand, "Help, I am a man, what is that?" and they withdraw: timidity. Two sides of the same medal, every man knows it.

Some reactions of some boys to the world around them, to the gender-specific role they have to play, to tile often caricatural pictures of manliness and to the rapidly changing society, may be at the expense of others (sexual violence, vandalism, small crimes, excessive risk behaviour, etc.), but these reactions are also at the expense of themselves and of each other. Nevertheless, boys also have certain qualities like strength, a true sense of responsibility, chivalry', directness, constructive forms of aggression, pleasure in pushing back frontiers and an urge to discover things. Only the premature & extra emphasis on exploring and autonomy and the lingering readjustment of gender-roles brings them off balance.

Social workers experience some problems with boys in various ways. Identifying oneself with the victims of violent behaviour by boys is almost a natural thing to do. The very idea that also boys can be victims of (sexual) violence is opposite to the general codes of masculinity: men rule, men can take a blow, can stand the pace, men take initiatives, men solve their own problems, *men are* never victims. But: facts and figures show that boys are more then girls at risk for violence outside, and inside families they are more beaten up than girls. It's also a known fact that boys more than girls act out stress. Traumatic experiences may be translated into aggressive behaviour, yet the opposite is seen as well: withdrawal.

Practitioners often find it hard that boys-in-trouble can express their own feelings and emotions only with difficulty. Or in a distant manner they even somehow identify themselves with the tough violent behaviour of some young men, becoming 'one of the boys' in such a way that they forget their pedagogical function (sometimes hidden in a liberal attitude, not wanting to be moralistic or even abdicating from every form of pedagogy).

'Working with boys' is not a reaction against working with girls. Yet, with all the sympathy felt for women's liberation as it developed in the Netherlands during the last decades, it is necessary to distance oneself a bit from it and – with respect for the position and interests of girls and women but based on the position of boys - to ask questions in order to make reflection on working with boys possible at all.

The central idea of the project is that young men are essentially responsible for their own choices and conduct. Understanding the roots of misbehaviour is never an excuse. If necessary firm boundaries must be set, and explained. But, if necessary within strong structures, other can help them to learn from their experiences, to look for alternatives, to project themselves into someone else's position and to broaden their options. Working with boys is before anything else a voyage of discovery with them in search of a new story on masculinity.

Boys can try to find out what they can win when they anticipate at a better spreading of their: energy and time over paid work. volunteer work, self-care, care for their environment, for their relations, for their partner and possible children, study and recreation.

After Japan and Korea, Holland has the highest productivity per hour, but this fact goes together with an extremely high discharge of anyone who is not capable for at least 120 % ....

A tendency in all rich countries, especially in the North-West of Europe. Focussing at paid work and career only, makes men very vulnerable. With too much stress in their twenties and thirties (the time when they get children) in search of promotion or material richness (and feeling the breath in the neck of younger ones struggling their way up), they get worn out in their forties and fifties. Material wealth functions as a compensation for the burdens that our society puts on the back of men, and as a symbolic sign of male success. Our economy 'flowers' on this principle. But: in the rich parts of Europe lots of people can't hold a paid job until their pension.

Many are excluded from this 'male paradise' long before. This observation is no echo from idealistic illusions in the sixties, but realistic from a human-resources point of view. Richer than ever before in many parts of Europe, many men and women get sick from overburdened or crooked-loaded are different. Better adjustment and spreading of energy gives both sexes a better balance in life, consequently less diseases and disablement.

Much (mis-) behaviour by boys as well as their timidity can be viewed as some sort of 'coping', 'survival-strategy' or 'solution' which boys adhere to in order to conquer - or escape - from the dilemmas or contradictions experienced by them. From this point of view there may develop an understanding of - and an insight into - a possible malfunction of boys and the motives behind their behaviour. This way of looking at boys may inspire professional workers to intervene more adequately and support the boys in some ways, to assist them in developing other behaviour, to prevent them from harmful habits and to block any misbehaviour. This may prevent much necessary grief among the boys themselves, not to mention their environment.

The social value of the project is to on the one hand 'equip' the boys - society's future men - more adequately to make a well-balanced contribution in work, care and self-care, and to 'equip' workers more adequately to support boys in achieving this aim. On the other hand the project should lead to a decrease of violence against girls and women and of other forms of aggression like vandalism, for example.

III. The aims of the project

The project has various aims concerning specific themes concerning working with boys. These aims are:

- To induce discussions about the basic principles of the project among professional workers and practice-oriented scientists closely in touch with the field in question.
- In almost the same movement, to develop and redevelop in a continuous way concepts on male aspects of socialisation, behaviour and societal tendencies.
- To describe and examine the existing ways of working with boys, and to offer suggestions to improve their gender-specific contents.
- To develop or to have more adequate methods developed in the broad field of youth work.

IV. Themes

Themes that have been dealt with in the past years - in co-operation with other professionals - are (among others):

- Boys and aggression (police, justice, direct and related alternative tasks to be carried out instead of punishment in terms of imprisonment).
- Prevention of sexual violence by boys. (among other examples the project is deeply involved in an advisory role in a large government supported campaign on TV and in classrooms, etc. for prevention of sexual violence.
- Social assistance to perpetrators as well as to male adolescent victims/survivors of sexual violence.
- Boys and work (breaking the fixation on work, developing one's self-confidence, insight into one's own skills, pleasure in working together, learning to

combine work and caring tasks).

- Allochtonous boys (for example Moroccan boys in the Netherlands are identified too quickly with problem descriptions, while they have their qualities as well).
- 'Among boys' (intimacy among boys, homophobia, ways of avoiding the impossible pair of notions of heterosexuality and homosexuality).
- Boys and intimacy/sexuality (open up communication, how do they feel about it, first experiences, ways of dealing with sex-differences and codes they are confronted with).

  Boys in field-social work (intake, first contacts, how to establish a working-relation, how to come further than just material help or relief).

Participation in some of these themes is to be continued. New themes since 1992 are:

- Boys in socio-cultural youth work: participatory research development in co-operation with local practitioners and their consultants.
- Boys in education (developing educational strategies on redistribution of paid and unpaid work between men and women, preparing boys for a better balance between various sectors of their life and between following episodes in their life).

Since 1992 there are also activities around adult males, for instance a training project for male general practitioners how to deal with sexuality, intimacy, limits in this field in their own practice.

Each practice aims at making one or more products concerning working with boys on the specific theme or the type of work in question, which have to meet the following requirements:

- It useful for professional workers in their practice.
- The product is an example of what working with boys may mean if one assumes the gender-specific character of the position and problems which boys have as described in the project.
- The product has to be new.
- The product should have a 'trigger' function: it makes visible and attractive what such a way of working can yield and should also stimulate a comparable development of methodology and/or work.

V. Means

In order to stimulate the discussions which should result in the development of more adequate methods, the project serves as an intermediary. An interactive network of expert workers and researchers is employed for the entire project and for each constituent theme or project, who sometimes participate free on the condition of an active own contribution. ('Balance of giving and getting'). For this purpose a large address- and information file has been built up and used widely. The work is done with persons and/or with organisations, but with some emphasis on the persons involved. Organisations can be positively influenced through their employees, who participate in the project because of their personal qualities, and through small conferences, one or a few congresses, advising, training, Consultancy, lectures and information. Furthermore, the project aims to have international exchanges, among others through study trips, possibly translation of products from other countries, offering lectures and workshops abroad, and participating in study conferences.

VI. Some further characterisation of ways of considering boys:

The views of the project can be represented in a practical way in a number of theses.

1 Every boy has his skills. Social work, youth work, residential care and police work are inclined to focus solely on problems. On what somebody cannot do, or where someone has gone wrong. Education can tend towards an explicit emphasis on what a pupil does not know. However, solutions to problems have to match skills that are already present. The learning process is also cumulative, it builds on what someone already knows. Therefore it is advisable to examine what skills or knowledge a boy possesses.

2 Much behaviour of boys - whether it is bravado or timidity - can be understood in the light of their attempts to master 'manliness'. It is a productive opinion to consider all types of behaviour, also misbehaviour, as a (if only symbolic) 'solution' or 'coping-strategy' to the questions, desires, dilemmas or conditions which they have. It is insufficient to only restrict misbehaviour. It is necessary to look over the shoulders of the boys and try to find other 'coping-strategies' or 'solutions' with them.

3 'Masculinity' and 'femininity' are social codings which do not fit each separate man or woman. Each individual is a unique combination of biological/genetical elements, experiences, qualities and skills. However, in the course of an age-long labour division according to sex, these qualities and skills have been tagged with the adjectives 'male' and 'female', which have become very influential.

4 Even the ticket 'boys' is a 'dangerous' category: every boy thank goodness is different. nevertheless, it is possible to develop ideas on frequently occurring behaviour and patterns of socialisation, a kind of comprehensive 'story' or masculinity and boys, that may guide us in our work with boys. It leads attention to certain clues. For example, it could be said that the behaviour of boys 'organises itself' within a broad spectrum with the extremes on the one hand being

bravado or boasting and on the other hand withdrawal (timidity). Nevertheless this does not relieve any practitioner from his responsibility to look over the shoulder of every boy he works with, and to research with them their world and their specific qualities and needs. A story like this must differentiate according to class, educational-level, ethnic culture, etc.

5 'Men do have the power', and it does not serve them well (neither their surroundings and environment)! So we need to look at this power: what does it exist of, and what are the motives behind it? Just sheer biologically encoded tendency to dominate? Keeping grip on a hostile world? Reducing nature to environment? Or reducing uncertainties because they are not raised in dealing with them? The thesis that men have the power in our society is true in many ways, but because of its over-simplification it prevents it prevents one from gaining insight into the relations between men and women. The used means of power and abuse of power is often related to feelings of impotence. When men (attempt to) exert power over their environment or over other men and women, this often has to do with feelings of impotence, humiliation or feeling threatened in some way or another. In mutual power relations men and women use different means of power. Boys grow up with these differences.

6 Boys can have difficulties with intimacy, because they find it hard to know and appreciate their own inner motives. The roots of this are to be found both in the socialisation of boys and in its social embedding. Many boys having difficulties in forming relationships, because the bond with the mother was interrupted too early without being countered by an everyday, balanced and emotional bond with the father (or men). The media and advertisements reinforce this process. The consequences are among others: feelings of loneliness, a weak ego, solving one's own problems and little introspection.

7 Women cannot learn from men how to be a woman, unless according to his wishes. In the same way boys cannot learn from a woman how to be a man, unless to her wishes or projections. Fathers or other men are often men are often absent in the childhood years.
Again: own experiments with manliness by boys are influenced and complicated by dominant images of masculinity, the absence or detachment of adult male examples, and by fellow-boys who also act is if they know the essence of being a man.

8 Manliness can be looked at as if it is a badly fitting coat. You bought the coat because there were no other coats in the racks or you think you will be laughed at in a uncommon coat, thus you adjust your posture in a way so that the coat fits, and after some time you think that it really fits, while in reality you limp.

9 Boys are, well-nigh in a structural sense, not raised in terms of empathy towards others. The consequences of one's own actions towards other is not the focus of attention for a 'real man'. In contrast with this, having an image, action, performance and 'scoring' are the characteristics of a 'real man' (a man is what he does and how he appears to the outside world).

10 In their search of what it is like to be a man, boys develop many qualities, 'guts' and much pleasure; they experiment and play with positions. It is an art in itself to appeal to these matters when working with boys.

11 High demands are good. Too much emphasis on work, career and material wealth as well as too high demands on boys make them vulnerable to fear of failure. Alternative networks, for instance those of small or big criminality, drugs and grey or black market, can then compete with the labour market.

12 Feelings of malfunctioning, not feeling part-of-it-all, can be compensated. Tensions can give the feeling to exist, to be alive. Organising 'kicks' and 'clicks' can be a substitute for a deeply rooted self-confidence. Various drugs and alcohol function in many ways in dealing with the tensions related to masculinity or help to suppress the demands of the outside world and / or breaking down barriers.

13 The essence of working with boys is to help them develop the skills they need to keep one's own in a world which burdens men one-sidedly, invests them with power and isolates them from intimacy, care and inner reflection: "It is necessary to achieve and succeed, if possible in the quickest and cheapest way; the consequences are for others ..."

14 In order to be able to work with boys in a constructive way, it's necessary that men and women know their own history, understand their own role and can cope with their own personality, as a man or as a woman. How did they become the man or woman they are now? Boys observe them, more than listening to them. Boys are anxious to find signals about what it is to be a man, sensitive concerning expectations and afraid to make a foolish impression. The principle of girls work – it has to be done by women – does not necessarily go for boys' work, given the fact that boys are from their socialisation familiar to women. Men as well as women can contribute to good work with boys, each in their own way.

15 Constructive working boils down to:
   a. Humour, play and challenges. If you haven't: go find another job.
   b. Being able to inspire confidence.
      This means that, to begin with, one should see what a bay can do well, his

qualities, and mirror it to them.

c. Being able to make a distinction between what a boy is (can be) and what he is doing. For example, don't say: "You bastard", but "You are behav ing like a bastard".

d. Blocking misbehaviour without any misunderstanding, and explain to the boys why this is done.

e. Confronting boys with the consequences of misbehaviour for themselves and for others.

f. Exploring their motives, desires, wishes and dilemmas with them and to help them develop their 'skills' and 'strategies' ("what do you really want, and how do you think you could realise this ...").

g. Challenging, stimulating, presenting interesting new tasks, in which they can discover their qualities.

h. Providing young men with richer images of manliness than the standard advertisements (the ads follow the dominant images which each of them also meet a particular, if not a pathological, need: caricature as they are, they both meet the need of certain images of manliness and they serve commercial interests).

i. Helping them proportion their behaviour and to take the responsibility for the consequences of their behaviour.

j. The golden key: Working on a real instead of an acted self-confidence. This means 'editing' situations, designing situations and being able to recognise the things or tasks that boys can carry out well, of which they can be proud, with which they can broaden their minds. (This cold also be putting a nappy on a baby or building a wall.)

Addendum to paper 'Boys between bravado and timidity' (This can be used as a hand-out, please distribute this among colleagues, LW)

Project 'Working with Boys' (Netherlands)

Development of conceptual models, innovation strategies and methods concerning gender-specific education and social work with male adolescents and adults; networking, lectures, training and consultancy.

Some short information about the project and the project leader

The project is an expertise-centre, being a part of the Hogeschool van Amsterdam, Faculteit Sociaal-Agogische Dienstverlening (Polytechnic College of Amsterdam, Faculty of Social-Pedagogical Service [Higher Professional Training in Social Work], formerly Karthuizer College of Social Studies). The project is engaged in

development of products in the field of gender-specific work with young men.
Key issues of conceptual research are: victimisation versus empowerment, redistribution of paid and unpaid work, sex and gender, qualities of men, male coping skills.
On the method side: the project aims at developing means of productive self-assessment of workers in the field of social work, youth work and education.
The project offers lectures, workshops, consultancy, & trainings, in the Netherlands as well as in other countries. Lectures, consultancy and trainings will be given in English, although to a certain extent communication in German and French is possible as well.

On request a paper on the project and a list of services and tariffs can be provided.

1) Cf. Conceptual research like 'Grounded Theory' according to Glaser and Strauss.
2) L. Woltring. 'Boys between bravado and timidity. Gender-specific work with boys' Culemborg, 1988, comprising a conceptual frame, interviews with successful practitioners, questionnaires, resources and some articles from Dutch writers as well as from England and Germany. It pays attention to various line of approach; developmental psychology, cultural-historical psychology of learning, socialisation and sociological dimensions. Until now only the title has been translated into English; more about this book in §6.
3) Written in Dutch, provisional title: 'It's up to me to decide! New directions in work with boys: youth work, education and social work'. With a review on the first book , a collection of practice experiences in various fields since 1988, clues and instructions for practitioners and a systematic questionnaire aiming at self-assessment and self-development of new methods by the practitioners.
4) Not to mention relapse in a violent fighting-identity as can be seen in some crisis-situations: Los Angeles! Former Yugoslavia?

2.4 User-Involvement in Social Services: Learning from Good Practice in Europe

Suzy Croft and Peter Beresford

Abstract.
In Britain two major developments are affecting the nature of social work practice, policy and education. These are the move to a mixed economy of welfare and the emergence of movements of disabled people and other recipients of social work services. Both developments emphasise a shift from' paternalism and dependency to independence and involvement for social work service users. These developments are also being experienced in other European countries.
The authors, funded by the Joseph Rowntree Foundation, have just completed the first British study of service user and local involvement in social services in Britain. This paper reports some of the findings from this study and argues for a European study to exchange information and experience on user-involvement in social services, as well as suggesting possible models for undertaking such a study.

User involvement in social services in Britain

There have been **two key developments** in welfare in Britain during the last ten to fifteen years. These have had profound implications for social work in the UK.

The mixed economy of welfare
The first of these developments has been the move to a mixed economy of welfare. Following the creation of the welfare state in Britain after the second world war, social services were dominated by state provision, although there were also smaller but significant roles for voluntary and commercial services. In the 1980s, state welfare services were called into question, first because of economic recession and reduced resources and then by ideological arguments for a new social economy with a much greater emphasis on the market place. There were many reasons for disenchantment with the British post-war welfare state. Most important among these was the rise of the political right and the election of Conservative governments from 1979 which were concerned about the cost of public services; disliked the 'nanny' welfare state which they perceived as creating and perpetuating dependency; were opposed to large scale government intervention and were committed to a greater role for the private market in social policy.

The emergence of disability and service user organisations
The second major development has been the emergence of groups and organisations of people who use social work and other social services. These include disabled people, people with learning difficulties, older people, people who use mental health services, young people in care and people affected by HIV. The. 1980s saw

these organisations multiply in numbers, size and effectiveness. These groups have developed their own critiques, their own ways of organising, their own programmes of demands and strategies to achieve them, and their own prototypes for services. Disabled people, for example, have developed a new politics of disability based on a critique of existing services, a redefinition of the problem and an attempt to create an alternative service and support structure controlled by disabled people. This followed from a social model of disability which emphasised that people's disability is caused by social factors, including the discrimination and oppression they face in society and not by their individual impairments. What disables people, they argue is their inability to function in an able-body oriented world which denies or does not take account of their rights and needs.

These groups and organisations are increasingly seeing themselves as new social movements, identifying themselves with other new social movements like those of women, black people, gays and lesbians and environmentalists. They point to their shared characteristics and goals.

From provider to user-led social services

These two developments have clearly inter-acted with each other, but they have also retained their own distinct perspectives and politics. They have many differences, but they have at least one emphasis in common, the importance both attach to moving from provider-led social policy and services to user-led social policy and services. What is meant by provider-led is that the providers of services, including politicians, managers, academics, researchers, planners and practitioners have shaped them, not the people for whom they are intended. So, for example, people have to fit into an existing pattern or framework of services rather than services being designed to match their individual needs. A number of key problems are associated with such provider-led services, including institutionalisation, paternalism, inadequate safeguards for the rights of service users, and abuse.

In Britain, successive governments have expressed their commitment to more user-led and user-centred services. They have placed an emphasise on the individual's rights of choice and exit from services as a welfare consumer and offered this as the rationale for their shift to a mixed economy of welfare and the restructuring of health and social services on the basis of the 'purchaser/provider split'.

Similarly, service user and disability organisations campaign for services which enable their independence by providing the kind of support want and prefer. They have pressed for and developed both individual personal assistance schemes controlled by disabled people and user-led collective services which they run and control themselves.

User-involvement

A central and unifying idea underpinning interest in more user-centred and user-led services has been that of user-involvement A growing view is that the switch to more user-centred services is likely to be achieved by making possible the increased involvement of people as service users. This is reflected in the arguments and activities of both the developments we have identified; government social policy and the emerging service user and disability movements. It is reflected in government legislation and guidance requiring user-involvement in both community care and child care. Both the National Health Service And Community Care Act and the Children Act place requirements upon public authorities and give rights to service users to be involved; to be consulted, to have opportunities to comment and complain and to be supported to do so.

Disability and service user organisations place an emphasis on people's participation. People are concerned with speaking and acting for themselves. Many use the term self-advocacy. This is a primary concern. It extends beyond the involvement of their constituency, to the active involvement of as many members of it as possible. It is an explicit expression of their concern with a different, more participatory politics.

These two developments, the marketisation of welfare and the development of new social movements of welfare service users and the increased interest in user-involvement that goes with them, do not seem to be confined to Britain. Economic recession, the election of right of centre governments and the collapse of communism in Eastern Europe, all offer comparable political and economic conditions elsewhere 1n Europe and beyond: There are also burgeoning disability and service user organisations and movements in Europe and elsewhere; as well as European and international organisations.

User-involvement, as we have said is central to these developments. It is currently a focal issue in welfare generally and in social work specifically. This has major implications for the practice, organisation and management of social work; social work training and social work research. In Britain all of these, particularly the organisation and role of social work are being profoundly affected by the changing requirements of government and the growing demands of service user and disability organisations. New roles are being created; new skills and different ways of working are required. For this reason, it seems helpful both to share experience in Britain and to raise the issue of exchanging experience from different countries within Europe. This is the aim of this contribution.

First we shall report the aims, methods and findings of a research project we undertook, with the support of the Joseph Rowntree Foundation, on user and local involvement in social services in Britain. Then we will discuss some possible aims and methods for work to exchange European experience of user-involvement in social services.

The research project

The research project we carried out had two aims. These were first to find out more about existing developments to increase people's say and involvement in British statutory and non-statutory social services, and second, to develop models and guidance to increase people's involvement and for improved practice for more participatory social services' policy and practice. The study involved'

- carrying out the first national survey of user and local involvement in statutory and voluntary social services;
- a search of participatory schemes and developments in personal social services;
- following up developments in other fields like housing, health and community developments which have helpful insights to offer;
- structured discussions with people involved in more than 80 selected participatory schemes and initiatives. These schemes included ones set up both by service users and service providers;
- a particular focus on the views and experience of service users;
- the production of practical handbooks for service providers and service users.[1]

Some of the key findings from the national survey were:

- Just under a third of social services departments and nearly half of the sample of voluntary organisations reported that they had formal policies to involve service users in the provision of their services;
- While there were many small scale initiatives and developments, there were few coherent or comprehensive schemes to involve service users;
- Greater diversity in the supply of services did not necessarily increase the involvement of service users. Such participation needs to be built into the way services are organised. Local authority and voluntary social services offer valuable lessons to the growing private sector about how to develop this involvement;
- Social services intervene to restrict as well as safeguard people's rights, for example in the case of child protection and where people are seen as a danger to themselves or others. Existing initiatives suggest that it is feasible and important to involve service users in both cases;
- Increasing people's involvement in social services has resource implications, but this does not necessarily mean more expensive services.[2]

The overall study raised some other key issues, which we would like to discuss in more detail. These seem to be of particular importance, both for understanding user-involvement and for encouraging and supporting its effective development. These issues include:

- the different interpretations placed upon 'user-involvement'
- two key components for effective involvement
- involving black people and members of other minority ethnic communities
- the importance of involving and empowering workers
- representativeness.
- service users as trainers

Two models of user-involvement

Let's begin with the first of these, the different interpretations placed upon user-involvement. There is no consensus about what user-involvement means. Two main interpretations emerged from our research. These are the consumerist and democratic approaches. They reflect the different pressures for people's increased involvement which we have already described; from government and from disability and service user organisations.

The consumerist approach to involvement has largely been developed by service providers and their organisations. Here the main aim is to improve the efficiency, economy and effectiveness of organisations and services. Service users, the argument goes, can help in this by contributing their ideas and experience to improve management and decision-making. The two kinds of involvement most closely associated with this approach are consultation and market research:

The consumerist approach is service centred. The term consumer describes people in terms of their relationship with a product or service. This approach places an emphasise on 'exit', that is to say, people's ability to turn to another service if they are dissatisfied. Power remains with services and their providers. people can feed in their ideas and experience but agencies still make the decisions.

The democratic approach is not service centred. It is concerned with people having more say and involvement in their lives, not just in services affecting them, although this is seen as important too. It is concerned with people's empowerment, with their civil rights, equality of opportunity and sometimes with the achievement of broader social change. The democratic approach has mainly been developed by service users and their allies. It aims to empower people by giving them a voice in organisations and services. Power and changes in the distribution of power are central to this model. It is concerned with people as citizens. The term citizen describes people in terms of their civil rights and relationship with the state. A democratic approach is most closely associated with schemes to increase people's direct involvement in decision-making. At present the dominant approach to involvement in community care and other public services in Britain is the consumerist, not the democratic one. There are also growing fears that concern to keep down expenditure currently counts for more in public services than meeting the needs of the consumer. There are overlaps between consumerist and democratic approaches to involvement, but there are also real differences. Both have strengths and 'weaknesses. What is important is not to confuse one with the other. People need to be clear what kind of involvement they want and what kind agencies are offering.

Two key components for effective involvement

Two components appear to be essential here if people are to have a realistic chance of exerting an influence and all groups are to have equal opportunities for involvement in social work services. These are **access** and **support.** Both are necessary. Experience suggests that without support, only' the most confident, well resourced and advantaged people and groups are likely to become involved. This helps explain the biased response that participatory initiatives have typically generated in Britain. Without access, efforts to become involved are likely to be arduous and ineffectual.

Access in the specific context of services, includes physical accessibility, the provision of services which are appropriate for and match the particular needs of different groups, and access points providing continuing opportunities for participation within both administrative and political frameworks and structures, including membership of sub-committees, planning groups, working parties and so on, as well as involvement in continuing information gathering and consultation exercises.

The need for support arises not because people lack the competence to participate in society, but because people's participation is undermined by or not part of the dominant culture or tradition. Users of social and other welfare services may also be particularly disadvantaged and disempowered. People may not know what's possible or how to get involved; may not like to ask for too much or be reluctant to complain. There are five essential elements to support. These are:

- *personal development:* to increase people's expectations, assertiveness, self-confidence and self-esteem;
- *skill development:* to build the skills they need to participate and to develop their own alternative approaches to involvement;
- *practical support:* to be able to take part, including information, child care, transport, meeting places, advocacy, expenses, etc;
- *support for equal opportunities:* provision for disabled people, people with sensory impairments, without verbal communication, non-readers, people for whom English is not their first language and people with intellectual impairments, to take part on equal terms;
- *support for people to get together and work in groups:* including administrative expenses, payment for workers, training and development costs;

Involving black people and members of other minority ethnic communities

Experience in Britain indicates that unless schemes to involve people ensure equal access to black people and members of other minority ethnic communities, they are likely to *increase* existing discrimination and possibly even legitimate, it instead of countering it.

All the indications are that is essential to make specific provision to involve members of minority ethnic groups. It is not enough to assume that they will get involved in the general run of things. Experience shows that this just does not happen.

There are three steps which agencies can take to promote anti-racist policy and practice to involve people. It is important that agencies

- pay particular attention to the needs of minority ethnic groups in making provision for people's involvement;
- provide resources to help service users' groups and rights organisations to reach out and involve members of minority ethnic communities;
- give specific support for minority ethnic communities to develop their own initiatives to increase the say and involvement of their members.

There are issues here for disability and service user organisations as well as service providers. In Britain, these groups are still often predominantly white. This may have a lot to do with the fact that services themselves have tended to be white-led. Two things are needed to change this:

- the development of anti-racist attitudes, practice and policy;
- resources to reach out and involve members of minority ethnic communities fully.

The importance of involving and empowering service workers

All the signs are that initiatives for user-involvement are likely to be more effective if workers and trade unions are actively involved in them. Social workers and other social services practitioners have played a valuable role as allies and advisers of user, disability and self-advocacy organisations. It is important that participatory schemes are developed in association with them. Imposing such schemes top-down is likely to undermine them. Service workers often have considerable knowledge of working in a participatory way from their day to day contact with service users. That experience should not be lost. If service workers are not involved they are unlikely to have any sense of ownership of participatory schemes and are in a powerful position to undermine and sabotage them.

There are important overlaps between service users and workers. They face some of the same discrimination. Disabled people are under-represented as workers in health and social services and women and members of minority ethnic groups are over-represented in low paid and low status employment. This makes it especially important for social services to involve rather than exclude workers, if they are not to reinforce the broader discrimination they face. Social workers will also need support to work in the more empowering ways which are now required of them.

User involvement and representativeness

In our research project, the reservation which we most often encountered from service providers against people's involvement was that they might be 'unrepresentative'. It went something like this: 'Who do they represent? What gives them a right to speak for people?, What mandate have they got?' Significantly this argument was rarely raised when other people spoke on service users' behalf, but it is frequently offered now that they seek to speak for themselves.

Representation poses some real problems. There are practical difficulties in the way of involving a broad range of people in any participatory activity. In Britain there aren't strong traditions of large scale involvement in political or civil activities. But questioning people's right to be involved on the basis that they are unrepresentative, can also serve as a convenient excuse for continuing to exclude them and for service providers to hang on to the power they have. It also ignores and denies the legitimacy of disability and service user groups as democratically constituted organisations.

What our study suggested was that final responsibility for ensuring that people's involvement is as broad-based and representative as possible lies with service providers not with service users. The proportion and distribution of people who become involved seems to depend crucially on the access and support that are provided to make it possible for them to become involved.

User-involvement in social services also highlights conflicts and contradictions between representative and participatory models of and structures for democracy. While service providers have often called the representativeness of-service users into question, the arrangements and structures which they generally provide for participation are representative ones, that is to say, they invite service user representatives to take their place next to service provider spokespersons and representatives. What this suggests is that service providers have not yet developed appropriate forms and forums to make possible the self-advocacy which service users increasingly demand, but still rely on arrangements for representation which may not sit comfortably with the new participatory politics of disability and service user movements.

Service users as trainers

Service users in Britain are now involved in many ways in social services. They are involved in assessment and in employing their own personal assistants; in running and planning services, in evaluation, quality assurance, contracting and staff recruitment. As we have already said, the new interest in user-involvement in Britain reflects profound changes in welfare ideology and economics and in the role and contribution of service users. Social services commentators frequently sum this up as signalling and demanding a different culture from social services, both in terms of the practice and organisation of social work and social services.

Training is seen as having a key part to play in this transformation. It is not just that new understanding and new skills are required from such training. A different sort of training is demanded to achieve this, a training which itself involves service users. Service user trainers are identified as 'powerful agent for change'[3] in developing more participatory social work policy and practice.

User involvement in social services and Europe

The importance of collating and exchanging experience

So far in this paper we have looked at the background to user-involvement in social services in Britain and discussed some of the experience, issues, and problems identified in our research project.

One of the difficulties that emerged from our study was the shortage of accessible information and guidance about user-involvement available both to service users and service providers. It was part of our brief to address this gap and certainly information is now becoming more generally available from a variety of sources. However, we found that while there was no shortage of experience in enabling people's involvement in social services and seeking to empower people, frequently this experience was just not recorded, disseminated or easily available to learn from. Similarly there seemed to be little cross-fertilisation of experience from different fields.

People involved in pioneering initiatives often don't seem to have the time or confidence to write about them. Expert accounts by researchers are sometimes too far removed from the reality to be helpful. The difficulties in drawing on existing experience in Britain may help explain the hesitant, often unprogressive nature of developments there on participation and user-involvement in social and other services.

The difficulties in collating experience within Britain are magnified once we try and build on experience more widely. Present knowledge of user-involvement in Europe seems to be largely piecemeal, impressionistic and inadequately disseminated. Useful contacts are being forged between service users in different countries (for example, the work of the Hamlet Trust between UK and Poland with recipients of mental health services), while the European Commission facilitates links between disability groups in the EC. There are now Europe-wide groupings of people with mental distress and disabled people. It is likely that useful models of user-involvement may be found in countries such as Sweden, Norway and Holland. Certainly the Scandinavian countries introduced client access to records policies earlier than did most EC countries. But these are assumptions that need investigating.

There is particular value in exploring user-involvement in social services in Europe now. While as we have seen, there is increasing interest in this issue, there are also still strong suspicions, fears and anxieties about such developments, especially on the part of service providers. This places a particular premium on exploring and developing clear and effective models and strategies for user-involvement so that the efforts of both service users and service providers to move beyond paternalistic policy and practice make the greatest possible progress.

Our basic premise is that there are experiences and initiatives in user involvement in European countries which properly understood, recorded and disseminated can help to advance policy and practice within different countries. A project exploring user involvement in social services in Europe could make this experience and emerging models of better practice more accessible to service users and their organisation and to service providers and service purchasers.

We can expect there to be a wide range of variables between different European countries which would make such a project particularly helpful. These include, for example, different:

- organisational structures
- traditions and approaches to participation and user-involvement
- social work roles
- legislation and guidance
- suppliers of services
- social work models and traditions

- scale and kinds of disability and service user groups and movements

Research Strategy and method

We have tried to outline here an initial research strategy and method. These are offered not as a predetermined proposal, but as the basis for further discussion, modification and development.

A number of core criteria inform this initial consideration of research to identify existing experience for user-involvement in social services in Europe. These are that:

1. Such a project would be explicitly designed to be of value to both users and providers of social services in Europe. It would not be conceived of in narrow academic terms as a comparative research project, with the usual uncertainties about the application and usefulness of the findings. There would be a dissemination and development component built into it.
2. The process of the project would seek to mirror the participatory nature of its subject matter. This would include regular and continuing user-involvement in the project itself.
3. The experience of the European Institute of Social Services at the University of Kent, with whom the authors have so far jointly explored this idea suggests that to be effective and practical, comparative studies across Europe need to be confined
   a) in terms of the number of countries involved and
   b) the subjects to be studied.

A participatory research method for a participatory subject

One method for undertaking such a research project with which the authors are familiar and which is particularly sympathetic to the participatory nature of its subject matter, is the search conference. The main phase of the project could entail organising and conducting such a search workshop in each participating country, involving both service users and service providers-involved in selected participatory initiatives. The detailed agenda of these workshops would be agreed in association with agencies involved in collaborating countries, with opportunities for local flexibility.

The idea of a search workshop/conference is to provide a forum for people sharing a common concern over a particular issue, but who approach it from different perspectives, for example, as a user or provider of services, carer or manager. The goal is to share information and experience, reach mutual understanding of the issue and a shared view of the possible future. Search conferences do not deny the differences between people and allow them opportunities they might not normally have to express and exchange their viewpoints. (See, for example, Building Better Futures: The Report of a national search conference on the prospects for community mental health care, MIND, UK [1989].)

The approach proposed is one which enables the direct involvement of all parties,

is sensitive to the needs of service users, allows a dialogue to develop and enables people to speak for themselves.
Experience in similar initiatives where such an approach has been adopted, for example, the workshops initiated by the National Institute for Social Work's on user centred services in the UK, in which one of the proposers was involved, highlights its helpfulness.[4]
Draft reports of these seminars could then be produced. They would seek to be 'user-friendly' to make them accessible and useful to both service users and providers in the participating countries.
This could be followed by a conference/workshop in one of the participating countries for both service users and providers, but also inviting people associated with pioneering participatory initiatives in the project countries. The purpose of this event would be to assist dissemination of the findings of the project, to offer service users and providers a direct opportunity to learn more about helpful work in Europe and to facilitate contacts and alliances between service users across Europe.
The final phase of the project could be production of an accessible report bringing together the experience and models of improved practice that can be drawn from participatory initiatives participating in the project.

Alternative approaches to undertaking the project.
Two different ways of undertaking such a project present themselves. Each has its strengths and weaknesses. We outline them here again as a basis for discussion.
1. The first is a partnership approach. Here the process would be to work in collaboration with partners identified in each participating country. Using this approach, for example, would entail meeting with partners to agree what work is done within the project countries, by whom, over what period of time and agreeing and Sharing the meeting of costs. Partners would each be responsible for the research in their own country.
Experience indicates there can be practical problems of co-ordination, over timescale and responsibility when working with partners in this way. It can take a long time to secure collaborators to undertake the work required and to negotiate for several countries to meet their own costs of participating in a European project, regardless of the importance and value of the project. However, they are likely to have local knowledge and affiliations and can share work and costs.
2. The second approach is for work to be co-ordinated by a worker based in one of the participating countries who has responsibility for establishing contacts and links in participating countries, organising and undertaking the research in association with local initiatives and writing up the research.
This approach would ensure consistency, and help ensure progress was maintained, but there may problems with language and limited local knowledge.
Perhaps a preferable alternative would be to establish partnerships in each participating country, without the expectation of them having the lead role in organising and funding local activities, but for a worker based in one participating country to

maintain close links and contact with them.

References

1. Suzy Croft and Peter Beresford, Getting Involved: A practical manual, Open Services Project and Joseph Rowntree Foundation, London, 1993. Peter Beresford and Suzy Croft, Citizen Involvement: A practical guide for change, Macmillan, London, 1993.
2. Suzy Croft and Peter Beresford, From Paternalism To Participation: Involving people in social services, Open Services Project and Joseph Rowntree Foundation, London, 1990.
   Social Care Research Findings No 9, User Involvement In The Provision Of Social Services, Joseph Rowntree Foundation, July 1990.
3. Vivien Lindow, Just Lip Service, Nursing Times, December 2, Volume 88, No 49, 1992, page 63.
4. The User Centred Services Group, Building Bridges - Between people who use and people who provide services, National Institute for Social Work, London, 1993.

2.5 Social Workers Facing Immigration Control and Deportation

Debra Hayes / John Ranson

This conference is called in the spirit of European unification. Co-operation between schools of Social Work should be welcomed as an opportunity to develop good practice in Social Work and its education across Europe. However, that process of "Europeanisation" that we are today engaged in developing has another side and this paper will explore the question "Europeanisation for whom?" We hope to show that in fact, many European residents will be excluded from the benefits of unification; forced to remain "outsiders" in their countries of residence - an exclusion which is likely to include restricted access to social welfare.

Immigration laws are not neutral. In theory they affect all foreign nationals in Europe. In practice they are aimed at particular groups of people. Their aim is to control the movement and labour of immigrants, migrants and refugees. The racism of immigration control across Europe can be seen historically. In Britain the 1905 Aliens Act's purpose was to control the entry of Jewish Workers fleeing Eastern Europe. In Britain in the 2nd half of the century, the controls have been largely aimed at black workers, impoverished by Britain's Imperial past.

The post war British economy had been dependant, not on short term migrant labour but on long term and permanent immigrant labour, which it imported from its ex-colonies. Since 1962, immigration legalisation in Britain has attempted to reconstruct this work-force into migrant labour and to some extent to "catch up" with other European countries which in the post war period, operated systems of migrant labour. The "Gastarbeiter" (guest worker) recruitment scheme in Germany being one example.

Between 1955 and 1966 the former West Germany made agreements with Turkey, Tunisia, Yugoslavia and South European Countries for such labour. France did the same with post-independence Algeria. These European residents have limited rights of residence and differing access to citizenship. German citizenship law dating from 1913 defines descent "by blood", rather than place of birth, so access to citizenship is almost impossible for the 6.5 million "foreigners" making up 8% of the population. The British Nationality Act of 1981 restricts the rights of residents to take up British citizenship and for the first time, broke the link that children born in the UK automatically acquired citizenship.

The actual numbers of people in Western Europe with limited rights of residence is open to question. The figures vary from 9 - 17 million, disenfranchised people, legally residing in it. These people are distributed unevenly, with France, Germany and Britain having the largest populations. In actual fact, they constitute a very small percentage of the population - but their limited rights have a broader affect. All black people in Europe are then held to account for their presence and particularly in times of economic crisis can be easily scapegoated. The denial of citizenship rights in fact, fuels the fire of racism, giving ground to the idea that only certain sections of the population have "a right to be here".

Prior to the single European Act, of course, these people did not have freedom of movement in the EEC, because that freedom extended only to EC nationals. For some time, there has been a drive towards the alignment of immigration laws in Europe e.g. carrier liability legislation, the screening of applications by spouses, asylum status restrictions and in visa requirements. In future non-EC nationals only means of entry will be short term, short contract "guest work". This will be enforced both at borders but also internally through the workplace and access to welfare.

> "Free movement of persons between the member states of the community is one of the basic freedoms instituted by the community". (European Commission Document - "Freedom of movement for persons in the EC 1982".)

Unfortunately for those EC residents without citizenship, this will not be the case. For them it is not an opening of the borders, but a restriction both from outside the EC and for a percentage within the EC, however long established or permanent their residency.

Significantly, entitlement to a whole series of welfare benefits is also linked to immigration status. In Britain this applies to unemployment and housing benefits as well as student grants and treatment in the "National Health Service". Historically advanced capitalism there is a relationship between nationalism and welfare. The Liberal Government of 1906 in Britain, which legitimised the state provision of welfare and laid the basis of the welfare state, made eligibility for benefits dependant on immigration status. The passing of the Aliens Act in 1905 denied the entry of Jews into the country, but Jews already in the country were to be excluded from proposed welfare reforms. The role of the state in promoting the "Health of the nation" also legitimised welfare as a nationalistic concept. "Undesirable immigrants" were those who could not show that they were in a position to support themselves and their dependants. This is a direct fore-runner of the present UK "Immigration Rules", preventing entry to these who may, "have recourse to public funds" or may in any other way become a "burden on the state". In addition, the Aliens Act gave the power to the state to deport those "Aliens" who

> "had been in receipt of any such parochial relief or been found wandering without ostensible means of subsistence or been living in insanitary conditions". (S. Cohen in critical Social policy - Issue 13, Volume 5, No. 1, 1985.)

The ensuing Liberal legislation, notably the Old Age Pensions Act of 1908 and the National Insurance Act of 1911, both made eligibility dependent on nationality criteria. Legislation in the inter-war years reinforced the link between entitlement and immigration status. The tightening of the link between welfare and immigration status meant welfare agencies had an increasing role in investigating the nationality and residence of applicants.

In the post war welfare state, concerns abounded about the need to protect the new welfare services from those coming in to the country to "secure the benefits of the Health Service". The beginnings of black immigration fuelled demands for new controls as existing legislation was not enough to exclude commonwealth citizens, not technically "Aliens". Ideological propaganda about "black people abusing benefits" has continued unabated since. International controls against black people in Britain and access to welfare began more or less simultaneously with immigration controls. The political 'significance of this is not simply the exclusion of some black people from benefits, but that all black people then have to prove eligibility. By 1976, Asian women attending anti-natal clinics In a Midlands city were routinely required to produce passports. In the same way unemployment benefit services impose restrictions on "any claimant who appears to come from abroad". London housing offices now ask for passports, so black people must prove their rights to housing.

Across Europe many residents without citizenship are excluded from a range of welfare benefits even though they may have paid contributions to those funds. In Germany at present, one in 12 jobs is held by a guest worker. The 1.8 million Turkish workers and their families create jobs, contribute to the GNP and account for 7% of the total tax revenue. Yet their own access to welfare is restricted.

We have then a situation whereby through the use of immigration control and more latterly the rights to citizenship in Europe, a historical and ideological rationale, rooted in racism, for the type, extent and accessibility of social work and welfare services to black people and their communities. For us this is a central challenge to modern Social Work practice and education.

'Good' practice might be difficult to specifically define but what it must surely be is anti-discriminatory and anti-racist. Antiracist practice must be good practice . Equally, social work operates today in an increasingly bleak political and economic climate, the burden of which, in terms of poor housing, unemployment and poverty, falls disproportionately upon black people. They are becoming the subject of harassment, violence and marginalisation in Capitalist economies unable to provide even for the modest aspirations of large groups in society. For us, social work has, and always will be a political activity - it can only become more so.

There are undoubtedly tensions in this analysis in that it is not necessarily the purpose foreseen by the state for the employment of social workers. However our view is that unless workers are prepared to challenge and fight personally and structurally they themselves effectively become part of the wider oppressive, racist state apparatus. Working with individuals and families under threat of deportation is in our view, central to anti-racist Social Work practice.

It was through working with black prisoners within the criminal justice system that we became aware of the processes whereby convicted individuals, either at court, awaiting sentence or whilst serving prison sentences, could be issued with a notice of intention to deport. We learnt that by committing a criminal offence, black offenders exposed themselves to the scrutiny of their immigration status and their right to residence in Britain. For some this has meant not only serving significant periods of imprisonment, but then to be punished a second time by threatened deportation - we call it double punishment. This is sadly not the only process by which individuals can be threatened with deportation. Imagine becoming involved as a social worker with a family with a child that has learning difficulties, then after some weeks or months quite suddenly the family are told they have overstayed their permitted residence in Britain. Of course once again it is black people who face the brunt of this legislation. What then is your role as a Social Worker' in this process? After two high profile public campaigns in Manchester by courageous prisoners, in which social workers were actively involved in 1991 in Manchester, the campaign Against Double Punishment was formed. It represents a partnership between local probation offices, a family support group and Manchester Immigration Aid Unit. The aims of the campaign were broadly threefold.

1. To support and sustain public campaigns of individuals feeling the threat of deportation.
2. To provide training and increase the legitimacy and knowledge for fellow workers working with such individuals.
3. To campaign more widely for the abolition in law to punish twice individuals convicted of a criminal offence.

We believe we have achieved some modest successes and made some international links with a sister organisation in France. The victories won by some against decisions to deport them is testament to the resilience and resistance of those black people, their families and communities. It is however indicative of the nature of this struggle that members of the campaign continue to do their work for it, in free time, unrecognised by their employers.
Indeed, it is also the nature of the terrain that black workers in the campaign have come to the attention of the authorities simply because of this work and been subjected to the same racist scrutiny and harassment by immigration authorities.
There are then a number of significant implications for us as the educators of social work students. Primarily we have responsibility to ensure that we equip students with the values, skills and knowledge to plan and deliver services that reflect the multi-racial Europe in which we live. An important part in this process we believe, is for students to have a clear understanding of the historical and political significance of immigration legislation and control. A control which has perpetuated images of black people as "outsiders".
Within the social work diploma at our University we have actively sought to move away form compartmentalising learning from opportunities in this area, rather we are seeking to expand and integrate immigration and deportation work throughout the various components of the curriculum. By means of introducing it as a theme for the year, we have been able to build links with the immigration aid unit, members of whom have led workshops on the issues facing social workers. Equally, stu-

dents have been supported and encouraged to visit an immigration tribunal, held in the city. By raising the students awareness and interest they have also affiliated to a current campaign involving a local family fighting the threat of deportation. In addition, we have developed formats in which students can examine immigration legislation and/or what kinds of support, advice or services might be required for an individual facing deportation. Furthermore, we see the potential to extend the issues within the curriculum, particularly in terms of work with families and child-care services and would welcome exploring these possibilities with you. For example, what kind of social work service might be appropriate for a family facing a decision either to remain resident in Britain or Europe whilst one of their number is deported or indeed contemplating leaving with the deportee in order to sustain and maintain themselves as a family in a new country. What salient skills and knowledge do social workers require in this situation?

Ultimately we hope that by introducing the issues around immigration and deportation across the curriculum and thereby looking at the most effective and sensitive delivery of services to black people; we can play a part in challenging orthodox and traditional models of social work theories and practice. If we wish to create courses that attract black candidates, social work education must be relevant and meaningful to them. If we are committed to anti-racist struggle, it is a challenge to which we must all respond.

2.6 Cultural-Social Work in Cooperation with Paramaribo

Pieter van Vliet

1. Introduction

I should like to talk to you today, about Surinam and the co-operation projects that the Hogeschool van Amsterdam has developed with Surinam.
First I would like to tell you something about Surinam: its location, the form of population and the general political and socio-economic situation in Surinam.
Then I shall go into the objectives and the meaning of the Surinam-projects for the Hogeschool van Amsterdam, next about financing the projects and finally, about the perspectives of the co-operation.

2. Surinam

Surinam is a former Dutch colony. It is about four times the size of the Netherlands and is located between Brazil and Venezuela on the north-east side of South America. Its neighbours are Guyana (to the west) and French Guyana (to the east). The country consists mainly of tropical rain forest; most of the estimated 300.000 inhabitants of Surinam live in the narrow, very fertile coastal strip in the north. Most of them live in or around the capital city of Paramanbo. You hear correctly: the number of inhabitants is only 300.000, the same as a medium town in Western Europe. This number has an added significance, in the knowledge that approximately 200.000 people of Surinam origin live in the Netherlands, almost two-third of which in Amsterdam. Practically everybody from Surinam has relatives in the Netherlands and people from Surinam living in the Netherlands, have relatives in Surinam. Most people from Surinam have come to the Netherlands after or around the independence of Surinam 1975, possibly with a premonition of the trouble awaiting Surinam.
As a result of 300 years of colonial exploitation the population of Surinam very heterogeneous. Main groups of population are:

- Creoles, descendants of slaves that were shipped from Africa to work on plantations, of which the women were often sexually abused;
- Hindu, descendants of the 'contract-labourers' brought in from India after slavery had been abolished in 1860;
- Javanese, brought, for the same purpose from another Dutch colony: Indonesia, after 1890, when India had an emigration-stop;
- Indians, the original inhabitants of Surinam, they live mainly in the interior;
- Bush Negroes, descendants of slaves that fled to the interior;
- furthermore a small group of Chinese and Europeans (or Bakra's) lives in Surinam, mostly descendants of Dutch plantation-owners.

Surinam society and also politics are organised according to ethnic dividing lines and operate on the basis of 'patronage' (clients, favouritism) and corruption, similar to what is now exposed in Italy.

After five years of independence under a corrupt generation of politicians, in which the economic climate deteriorated, left-wing military took over power after a fairly peaceful coup in 1980, initially with the benefit of the doubt of the majority of the Dutch as well as the Surinam population. Most of the left-wing intellectuals were to some extent -enthusiastic about the coup, that brought a new revolutionary fire, as a consequence of which the country would be rebuilt with a number of socialistic ideals and would finally be able to shake off its neo-colonial inheritance once and for all.
When in December 1982, 12 opponents were killed by the military regime (the first political deaths for decades), the sympethatic attitude changed instantly. The Dutch government immediately ceased the generous annual development funds, that were agreed upon during the independence treaty and in the Netherlands the resistance against the 'Bouterse-administration'(leader of the military coup) was organised. When also the world market for bauxite collapsed, the situation clearly became untenable. Surinam export depended for 75 % on bauxite.
The economy collapsed, inflation was artificially controlled, which caused the black money market to take East European forms, resulting in great wealth for a small group of money merchants in a short time, at the cost of a deepening of the economic crisis. Soon there was not much left of the once so prosperous colonial country, the tropical paradise.
To make matters worse, the former bodyguard of commander Bouterse also started an actual guerrilla-war in the inhospitable interior of Surinam, which lead to near-Civil war and a veritable migration of the inhabitants of the interior, with the accessory refugee problem.
Over the past years there have been regular reports by particularly American intelligence services about the cocaine traffic in Surinam; it appears to be one of the major transit countries of Colombian coke.
Under pressure of circumstances the military renounced part of their power in 1989 and there were free elections, as a result of which the old guard resumed their parliamentary seats. The military had and still has an important part of the power and today there is a fierce fight over power, between the first president of a generation of politicians and the military authorities.
Surinam is in a state of deep economic and political crisis. Although it is a very fertile and relatively rich country with a small population and a tight connection with the Netherlands, the solution to this crisis is not yet in sight.
It is estimated that yearly + 40 million Dfl. of private help alone, such as goods and food parcels, is sent from the Netherlands to Surinam. In addition to this there is about 1,2 milliard Dfl. of frozen development money waiting for a good cause in Surinam. The first impression is, that with a bit of good (political) will an energetic policy, it should be possible to transform Surinam into relatively prosperous country on a short-term basis.
Several complex historical and political causes can be indicated for the unsuccessful attempts to fight the economic crisis.

Suffice it to say that there are apparently too many (powerful) people and groups that find it in their interest to let the current crisis situation continue and at the same time the concrete balance of power in Surinam is such that the current government has no, or at least not enough possibilities to take action against this.
With a grant from the Economic European Community a redevelopment plan was drawn up in connection with crisis control, by the consultancy firm Coopers & Lybrandt, that will have far-reaching social consequences; particularly for the socially vulnerable part of the Surinam population. The Netherlands have set as condition for resuming the payments of the development funds, that the redevelopment measures that were suggested by Coopers & Lybrandt are implemented unabridgedly.
During the last few months there has been an increasing interest for Surinam from Dutch politicians. Next to an extensive parliamentary delegation, several ministers, with on their trail an entire string of civil servants have travelled to Surinam for discussions about possible continuation of the ceased development aid. The Dutch preference is more and more obvious, to spend the development funds on project that concentrate on dealing with the social consequences of the redevelopment operation.
In this the Surinam social work will certainly play an important role.

3. How the Surinam-project at the HvA came into existence

Students from Surinam and the former Netherlands Antilles have studied at our school and its legal predecessors for years and years. At the time we estimate that 8 to 10 % of the student population in the Social Work department is of Surinam or Antillian descend. They are very much involved with the orientation of the 'motherland', just like the rest of the Surinam and Antillian people in the Netherlands. Many of these students cross the ocean on a more or less regular basis for a holiday or to visit relatives, and a number of them spend a practice period in connection with the education, in Surinam or the Antilles.
More and more, also Dutch students are interested in spending their practical training period in Surinam or the Antilles. At school and in the professional practice there is an increasing confrontation with people from Surinam and the Antilles and with their cultures, which results in curiosity about these countries and a desire to get better acquainted with this culture.

Contact with Surinam.

In view of this, a delegation of the Hogeschool went to Surinam, in order to reinforce contacts with the 'stage centrum' (practical training centre), make new contacts and to try to find new practicum settings. This initiative and the following intensifying of contacts with Surinam have lead to the request of the Stage centrum Paramaribo, to the Hogeschool van Amsterdam for a national co-ordination point, in order to co-ordinate recruiting, selection, supervision and support of Dutch students that want to spend a practical training period in Surinam. Meanwhile this co-ordination point has acquired a leading position, to full satisfaction of the higher

vocational educational schemes that avail themselves of its services.
In 1991, in consultation with the management of AHKO, the Surinam-Desk HvA, established to co-ordinate the rapidly expanding activities in Surinam, developed a number of project plans and presented them to the Dutch government for financing. These projects were carried out in the first six months of 1992, during three working visits to Surinam.
Apart from training and courses for supplementary training and support of Surinam social workers, this involved support activities for small-scale employment projects for women, organisation and consultancy for the Surinam Ministerie van arbeid (ministry of of labour) and research was made into possible 'co-operation and support in the health care sector.
At the time the HvA, particularly in the wide area of the social sector, has many excellent contacts with a number of organisations and several ministries in Surinam. Many plans and initiatives have been developed within the co-operation with these 'counterparts', and are now waiting to be carried out.
Recently we have also made excellent contacts with social work institutions on Aruba and Curaçao, two islands off the coast of Venezuela, belonging to the Netherlands Antilles, also a former Dutch colony. Because similar activities were planned there (and partly carried out) we nowadays speak of the 'Caribbean desk' of the Hogeschool van Amsterdam.

4. Framework in content and objectives of co-operation with Surinam and the Antilles

- **Interculturalization of education and anticipation of the multi-cultural society:**
  The 'multi-culturalisation' of society sets new standards for the professional practice and consequently for the Faculty's education.
  Inter-culturalisation of education is necessary in order to train students adequately to be professionals that are capable to find answers to modern .questions and problems. Among other things this will require students to develop multiple ethnic loyalties and to play the part of 'cultural mediator'.
  When we speak of the 'multicultural society', it must be considered, that people with a Surinam or Antillian background, in quantity alone, constitute an important element in this, certainly in the Amsterdam situation. Moreover applies for the Antillian and Surinam community, that they can not be understood without concretely involving Surinam and the Antilles.
  It goes without saying that Surinam and Antillian students want to be able to recognise themselves in the educational offer, actual knowledge and concrete concern for Surinam and the Antilles by the faculty, are of the utmost importance. Moreover, in a number of cases students want to go into the problems of the Surinam or Antillian society. Usually with the intention to deal with these problems, after completing the study, either in Surinam and the Antilles or not.

The possibility to spend a practice training 'overseas', should be maintained if not expanded for this reason alone.

- **Development co-operation**

  The Hogeschool van Amsterdam from its own social responsibility has the opportunity to contribute towards the (social) development of Surinam and the Antilles. This co-operation will focus on the the development of education and welfare and health care in Surinam and on the Antilles. In view of the nature of the projects, many of them could be eligible for financing by a third party.

  A large number of activities with regard to the Surinam and Antillian community have been realised in the meantime. However, with this the Hogeschool van Amsterdam is still far from multi-cultural (or international). The new faculty will certainly need her innovative abilities here.

  By her actions the Caribbean Desk intends to contribute towards the innovation that is necessary to realise a multi-cultural Hogeschool, in which every group of students will receive the education that suits them.

  Such an innovative effort should also be seen as the contribution the faculty can and should make to social problems in the closely knit Dutch, Surinam and Antillian communities, especially of course in areas within the faculties competence.

  This implies, among other things, direct care, support and stimulation of Surinam and Antillian students in finding their way to, in and after the education in the faculty.

3. Der Austausch von Studierenden und Lehrenden im Netzwerk der Hochschulkooperation

3.1 A Framework of Teaching Comparative Social Work

Kate Brown

Mobility

Service users and workers are increasingly likely to move between countries especially within the EC. As we move, we carry with us assumptions about what is normal welfare provision and therefore what we can expect from any system in any country.

When faced by the fact that other countries offer different services, organised in a different way with different priorities, workers and users tend to react sceptically, defensively or in amazement. How odd that social workers in Germany work in youth clubs; how awful that child benefit in Russia is only 50 pence; the only way that the Danes can afford such high levels of service is through punitive taxation; what a peculiar curriculum schools of social work have in France etc.

For migrant service users, the danger is that services will not be used if it is not known that they exist, or conversely that users will anticipate services which simply do not exist or are offered in a very different way and will become confused or angry.

We need to consider seriously the fundamentals of welfare provisions if we are not to over simplify or over generalise.

If we are to avoid generalised assumptions and false assumptions we need to know more about other systems, what they offer, how they are organised, what the underlying ideologies are. The best place to start this learning process is during the training of social work professionals or within social policy academic courses.

Learning from each other

Academics, students and social workers from one country can exchange experiences and research findings with their colleagues in other countries and thereby gain a more profound understanding of their subject area. By looking at alternative ways of approaching the same or similar problems we can deepen and widen our understanding of the significance of culture and of context. Comparative studies force us to look at the context of social welfare provision, which is all too easy to ignore when we are simply looking at our own system which we treat as a given truth.

If we know more about other systems there is a slight chance that we may use this when we need to change our own. We can swap intuition and inventiveness in dealing with social problems and perhaps become more creative collectively. Unfortunately, we tend to be very nationalistic in our approach to welfare provision. Our systems are rooted in our history and there seems to be a fear that if we take an idea from abroad it is not good enough. There are of course exceptions to this. The English seem willing to import American social work theories perhaps because of an apparently shared language but are reluctant to take views from nearer countries which are considered more foreign because of language differences, i.e. continental Europe.

The development of the European Community from a purely economic to a more social movement heralded the chance of greater interchange of ideas about social policies and welfare provision (eg the Social Charter) but this progress was paralleled by economic recession which has enabled the re emergence of new right wing political forces throughout Europe which in turn may well increase the nationalistic introspection of each country and decrease the internationalism which had at least begun in the EC.

On the other hand we as ex colonialists seem very willing to export our welfare systems along with our models of criminal justice to our old empires. Eg Fiji has a system of personal social services very much based on the English system and I have no doubt that if I were fortunate enough to go island hopping in the Caribbean I would find that each country's system could be traced back to its old colonial roots. The External Assessor for the Diploma in Social Work courses at the Manchester Metropolitan University is currently engaged in setting up social work service provision in the Seychelles.

Learning through confronting difference

By studying other peoples systems we are likely to learn more about our own system as well. By identifying differences and commonalties in provisions, priorities and methods of provision we can understand the purposes and meanings given to social welfare activities in each of the countries involved. When we encounter something which we find curious, hopefully we will sit back and think about our preconceptions and why we think as we do, not simply dismiss another approach as outlandish. My experience over 15 years of international exchanges is that students when faced with a very different system will initially think it is either very stupid or quite brilliant. They then start to question why the systems are different and to think through the reasons for the disparities. In doing this they think through the basis of the English welfare system as well as wondering why others do things differently.

Problems of Comparative Welfare Studies

What do we mean by social welfare?

There is no agreement, national or international, about what constitutes social welfare and social work. We can spend a lot of time arguing about definitions rather than getting down to trying to understand what each country provides and why.

Students are less interested in an academic debate about the constituents of welfare than they are in what benefits and services are available to a child with a physical impairment in any given country or what advice and assistance is available to a

pregnant fourteen year old girl. The debate about the meaningfulness of statistics or the exact interpretation of words can wait until we have a greater understanding of what aid is available. I would argue that students are more likely to come to a deeper understanding of the meaning of social welfare through an investigation of services provided in different contexts than they are to understand what it means through an approach which just relates the history and current provision of welfare services in their own country.
However, we can take as very loose guidelines that our studies of social welfare services should include

- education
- health
- housing
- income
- maintenance
- personal social services, which includes preventative services such as youth work alongside remedial social work for those already in need of service provision.

We should remember at all times that the English view of social work is a much more narrow one that in most other European countries where the distinctions between social work and, for example, social security, health visiting, youth work, occupational therapy, play therapy, counselling and community work (to name but a few) is considerably less restricted.
We should also bear in mind that social welfare systems are changing rapidly due to economic recession, the reconstitution of the formerly federal communist countries into independent capitalist states, and continent wide political shifts to the right. What appears in the text books may be out of date before it is even published.

We should also remind ourselves that in some instances our welfare provision may be more akin to that in the developing world than what we call the advanced capitalist countries. For example, day care for young children in England is more comparable with the third world than the rest of Europe where kindergarten facilities are commonplace.

SOME VARIABLES WHICH CAN BE USED TO HELP ANALYSIS CREA TING A FRAMEWORK FOR UNDERSTANDING COMPARATIVE STUDIES

Questions can be asked under the following headings in order to understand the welfare provision of any country. When attempting to analyse any social welfare or social work provision these questions are the minimum to be asked.

1. WELFARE IDEOLOGY

What is the basic welfare ideology of the country under consideration? How are social welfare services funded and provided? This is clearly a question which seeks to understand the political and value systems of the country.

According to Mischra (1) there are three major approaches to welfare at present

* social corporatism where the government and people uphold the view that the state should provide welfare services and that the cost of these services should be met before that of all other services they require such as economic or defence policies. Eg health services come before interest rates.
* new right which stresses the pulling out of the state from any but the most residual welfare provision, leaving all other welfare services to be purchased by the individual from wages, insurance or benefits.
* welfare pluralism/mixed economy of welfare which is fashionable in many countries where the cost of welfare benefits has become expensive and in countries which are beginning to move away from total non intervention to provide some selected welfare benefits. In these countries there is a mixture of state and private or voluntary provision.

With regard to income maintenance, Hill (2) argues that in Europe there are "two principal and differing traditions in social assistance, although over the years each has acquired some features of the other to become more hybrid:

* the Bismarckian approach popular in continental Europe focuses on generous employment based rights and social insurance, but with weaker rights for those outside the labour market. Benefit entitlements are based on occupational groupings, whilst rates of payment are usually in proportion to earnings for periods of economic inactivity including retirement.
* the Beveridge or Anglo-Scandinavian model concentrates on universal benefits financed largely-from taxation. system relies more on flat rate payments."

Many countries are struggling to decide what is the proper mix of state, voluntary and commercial provision as against family provision, self help, neighbours etc.
Many countries have a system/philosophy of subsidiarity which means that a larger unit is not expected to do what a smaller unit is capable of doing. This means that the 'church/community/commune will not do what the family can reasonably be expected to do. The local authority will not do what the commune could reasonable be expected to do and so on through regional and state government. This leads to an expectation of family provision or payment for services.
Where formal services do not yet exist, as in many developing countries it will be more difficult to establish any services as state owned even where the government so wishes because of the history of family responsibility and because the countries to whom they may look for finance will not approve high levels of state interven-

tion.
Most countries which have had a social corporatist, high cost services, especially residential services are moving towards closing or privatising services. Decarceration is put forward as the ideal. Community care is the model of the 21st century but usually without the finance to back it. Italy's apparent success in emptying the psychiatric hospitals disguises a lot of what we might consider unprofessional practice, like drug dispensing without the permission of the service user. Community care is often the harbinger of private practice.
As noted above, we should bear in mind that the text book writings about any country may be outdated. But using the most up to date knowledge we have we should ask the following questions:
*Is there a trend away from government provision and towards voluntary/private/commercial provision of services?

* Is the social worker involved in
    1. the direct provision of services to the service user?
    2. acting as agent on behalf of the user in purchasing the services from oth ers perhaps later inspecting that the services are being properly provided?

* Does the central or local government deliver the services or pay for them? Eg in Holland most social workers work for voluntary agencies but the government pays virtually all the costs, i.e. contracting out or franchising. Cf. Poland where the bulk of social workers work directly for the state.

* If the state does not deliver or pay for the services how are they funded? Through insurance? We should not assume that countries where services are purchased by the user either directly or through insurance have fewer services. The significance then becomes the ability to pay which may depend on the levels of social security payments.

2. ECONOMIC POSITION

Obviously some countries have more money than others. Most countries are in economic decline or stagnation. Where this is true then the provision of welfare services is likely to suffer unless the welfare ideology is so strong that it ranks higher than other economic needs (see social corporatism above). Even in Sweden, which 'has always been held up as the most obvious example of a country with a' proper welfare state, welfare benefits are now in decline.
However, it is still likely that choices will have to be made between competing interests. eg is it more important to educate children or to provide child benefits. eg Egypt has no system of family allowances although it does have a strong system of family planning services. But every child in Egypt is entitled to free education up to and including university level.

We need to ask the questions:
* What is the current economic position of the country? it deteriorating or improving?
* How much money is spent on welfare services?

3. DEMOGRAPHIC FACTORS

Population trends vary throughout the world but at present we can generalise that northern and western countries have a declining population where the numbers of elderly people exceed the numbers of children. In Europe, only Ireland has an above replacement birth rate. This means that in a few years time we will not be able to provide services for our elders unless there is a radical shift in our thinking about how to do it. When we add to the demographic problem that of the economy, i.e. the fact that those of employable age cannot find work and are therefore also dependent on benefits, we have a time bomb on our hands.
Those of us who will be 60 in 20 years time will not have enough young people to look after us not enough tax payers to pay for us to be looked after.
This contrasts with southern and eastern countries where the birth rate is far higher than replacement and the result is starvation or ecological disaster.
One solution may be an increase in immigration to Europe in order to balance the population and to meet the needs of European elders but we do not have a very commendable history of handling immigration. An alternative would be the emigration of the elders to countries where they can live more cheaply and receive services which they can pay for. We are already witnessing this in the form of the "Costa Geriatrica" in Spain, populated by English pensioners.
The welfare W. Welfare services are used at their maximum at three points in the life cycle and at their minimum at two intervening stages:

High	Infancy/childhood		young family		older age
Low		early adult		late middle age	

We need the population balance to pay for the services, those needing least services paying most.
We need also to consider the geographic distribution of the population, urban and rural factors. Most people outside Europe live in rural areas which are more difficult to service with formal personal social services. Such geography leads to different expectations of family commitments, whereby families need to support each other and to different levels of prosperity. However, this should not permit us to use peoples previous poverty and self sufficiency In a racist way which argues that they have always looked after their own so they can carry on doing so. Landless people are the poorest worldwide. But rural landowners unless they own a lot are also poor.

We need to ask the questions:

* What is the demographic shape of the population and where do the potential pressure points exist?
* Are there new population considerations?
* Is this country easily serviced or is the geographic distribution of population a problem to welfare services?

4. RELIGIOUS/IDEOLOGICAL DEMANDS

Some countries have a system of belief which requires them to give money and goods to those who do not have them. Zakat in muslim countries requires everyone to give surplus-income and goods to the needy. It is continued by giving part (approximately 2.5%) of the surplus to a charity organisation.
This charitable giving is seen by many outside the system as demeaning to those who receive it as goods but perhaps as less humiliating when the money is used to provide services. eg Germany has a system of church taxes whereby people pay a proportion of their income to a church charity which means then that the church is responsible for much of the social work provision in Germany.

We should ask the questions:

* To what extent is religious belief part of the building bricks of social welfare provision?
* Is the giving and receiving of charity viewed negatively or positively?

5. THE NATURE OF SOCIAL WORK

Any quick overview of service provision in Europe shows that what is considered social work in one country may not be seen as social work in another. In some countries social work includes what the English would see as health work eg France or youth work eg Germany or social security, eg Denmark, Holland, Portugal or sport eg Switzerland. The English perception is very limited usually to work which is paid for directly or indirectly by central or local government, which Cannan et al (3) describe as "concerned mainly with the relief of poverty and with individual need and deviance". Is there any reason to think that the work done by for example, personnel officers or occupational therapists or community workers or health visitors or counsellors is not more akin to social work as we know it than it is different. Are people who charge a fee (like most social workers in USA) or who are paid by the employer of the service user (like in many European countries including France, often called welfare officers in England) not social workers. The area covered by personal social services usually includes the personalising of the provision of the other welfare services.
There is also the whole profession of pedagogy which is not known in England but which is wide spread in Europe and, since Paulo Friere has become the preferred

model in many southern countries although Friere has a different emphasis from my understanding of much of pedagogy in Europe.
Social work can also be analysed through the user groups is works with: elders and their carers, .families with young children including abused children and adopted or fostered children, people with mental health problems, people with physical and mental impairments, people with health problems which may include substance abuse, offenders and their families etc. With all of these groups of users the social worker seeks to protect the civil rights of the vulnerable, to support and care for those in need and to provide social control by enforcing rules, laws and norms.
The nature of social work is changing throughout Europe in particular. We need look only at the restructuring of social work training which has occurred recently in both the Netherlands and Great Britain to see that. Some would argue that social work is under threat of extinction and certainly we are all faced with reviewing what we see as its essential nature. The power base of old forms of social work is certainly being challenged from inside and outside the profession. The emphasis has shifted, particularly in British social work training to seeing social work as tackling power, oppression and discrimination.
Here the language of social work is about user choice, user participation, empowering and tackling injustice. Social work is being judged from outside by criteria of effectiveness, efficiency and cost accountability, with greater emphasis on remedial tasks with the consequent loss of preventative work with families and communities, whilst on the inside social workers despair of the lack of resources and political will to meet the needs of the poor and disadvantaged.

The questions we need to ask when we seek to understand what social workers do in any country are:

* What group of service users does the social worker mainly work with?
* Who employs the social worker and where does the funding come from?
* What training did the social worker have?
* Where do they do most of their work? Office, users home, residential or day care establishment, club, hospital, on the street etc?
* What would the social worker describe as the main aims of the job?

USING A CASE STUDY APPROACH

Students can be encouraged to explore the nature of social work provision through the use of case studies.-
In my teaching of comparative social work I have used the framework which I have described above and related it to particular case studies of people in need of personal social service provision.
Last year, for example amongst others, we examined in detail in class:
the social work services available to a young, black man who had committed an offence in England and compared this with those services available to a young abo-

riginal man in Australia.
services available to children with profound deafness in England and compared it with the Netherlands and Denmark.
day care services available to pre school in England and Sweden.
Students were asked then to produce a case study example for assessment, the outline of which is attached. They had to choose a situation which would receive the attention of a social worker in one country and compare it with what would happen in another country. The resulting case studies were of a very high standard and students said that they gained a great deal from undertaking the task, both in knowledge about other systems and about English systems. They appreciated the space to think about why we in England have the approach to welfare which we have and enjoyed the challenge of thinking about why others do things differently.

COMPARATIVE SOCIAL WORK.

Word limits.
Diploma in Higher Education: 2000 words Master of Arts in Social Work: 3000 words.

This assignment requires you to-demonstrate an understanding of the provision of social work services in a self selected area of interest in two countries; to describe and analyse differing forms of service provision; to evaluate the implications of the services for the service users.
N.B. You must select England and Wales as the named country in either Part Two or Part Three.

Part One.
In no more than 200 words, develop a scenario which in one named country would involve the provision of formal social work services. This should involve the description of an individual, family or group which is involved in the use of assistance to solve a personal or social problem.
Part Two.
Describe and critically evaluate the sources and provision of services to the user/s as outlined above in the first named country.
Part Three.
Describe and critically evaluate the sources and provision of services to the user/s in one other country.
Part Four.
Present an evaluation in report form, which may involve the use of tables, flow charts etc, of the significant differences or similarities between the two countries and indicate a personal opinion as to the implication of these for the service users.
Part Five for MA students only.
Identify and analyse the historical and ideological roots of the provision of social

work services to users in the two countries.

Marking Scheme.

Dip HE		MA	
Part Two	30%	Part two	20%
Part Three	30%	Part three	20%
Part four	40%	Part four	30%
		Part five	

1. Mishra R. The Welfare State in a Capitalist Society Harvester Wheatsheaf 1990

2. Hill Malcolm (ed.) Social Work and the European Community Jessica Kingsley Publishers 1991

3. Cannan Crescy, Berry Lynne & Lyons, Karen Social Work in Europe Macmillan 1992Margri

3.2 Differences in Understanding Methods – Experiences from a Teacher's Exchange

Margrit Brückner

1. Some observations in comparison between the Netherlands and Germany

The idea of talking on methods developed during several discussions with students and staff of the Hogeschool in Amsterdam. First I would like to present the incidents that made me aware of the differences in dealing with methods, especially the, way how they are related to various standings on the notion of closeness and distance. Then I would like to present some ideas on what needs to be taken into account before being able to discuss the use of methods effectively demonstrated on research. results on understanding work concepts in women's projects.
When I taught social work students in Amsterdam for a month last year on questions of power and powerlessness of women in social work and other topics my conclusion was: Had I known the students' self-understanding as social workers beforehand, I would have discussed with them from just the opposite viewpoint of looking at interaction processes in social work as I actually did and as I usually do in Germany. Whereas German students tend to identify very closely with the fate of their clients, thereby running into problems of overestimating their influence, their closeness, their possibility to help and the necessity for immediate help - all of which tends to leave them rather helpless - the Dutch students informed me that they know about the importance of professional distance, about contracting and about the use and the value of methods. That again gave me the feeling, they might need to know more about the emotional side of working in the social field. I got this idea after having had several discussions on their social work activities with them and after a number of case presentations by them. Putting it in another words: whereas I think that literature and discussion on the problem of closeness, the dangers of mothering and identifying too closely with the client is of great importance for German students, I would suggest discussing with Dutch students topics like the limits of professionalisation, the unconscious side of methods and the inevitability of emotional involvement in the fate of the clients. How big the actual *differences* in *practical* terms are at the end between the Dutch and the German students I know is hard to say without doing *more* profound comparative work on it. But to make it more clear what I am trying to say so far according to my observation, I want to give two examples.
When I was in Amsterdam on a women-students exchange program the Dutch students gave papers on their practical work with women and girls. One paper was on the development of a detailed feminist *questionnaire* for first interviews with women coming to counselling. This questionnaire was seen as an *instrument.* of *better* understanding of the women and her problems and as a possibility to get a better *picture* of her life-situation to be able to help more efficiently. All this was

not so much said as taken for granted by the Dutch students.-Whereas by looking at the listening German students and the expression on their faces I could tell that they were very puzzled by the idea of a feminist questionnaire,- because to them a questionnaire was an instrument synonymous with exerting power and control over others. So one way of looking at this method was taking the woman serious and therefore needing to know -as much as possible about her and her life in order to find out the right Ways to help, the other assuming that this method was a means of control..

Something very similar happened when another Dutch student spoke about a progressive girls home where she liked to work in and where good work was done to help the girls. In this home they kept. something like a notebook in which the strong and weak points of behaviour of each girl concerning the ability to take care of herself was put down. The weak points were discussed regularly with the girl trying to find ways together to improve on them. At the same time the points were added up to decide on the amount of time and control needed for the girl. And there were margins set up for XXXX to the number of points which meant living on different floors of the house – the higher you get the less you are supervised and the more freedom you have. Again the Dutch students spoke with great certainty about this method, suggesting it being part of a valuable procedure – without showing any feelings of guilt (as I would have expected from a German student since she would interpret it as a form of control). The German students reacted in fact surprised because they did take it as an authoritarian measure, which they themselves would not use and when used in the institution they work in feel guilty or at least ashamed about.
I wanted to give these examples as an introduction into an ongoing research project in Frankfurt at the Fachhochschule on "qualification requirements and work profiles in women's projects". The question that interests us is the interaction process between project workers and women or girls and the ways and methods used to structure this process and the definition of the work contract. So far there exists only a vague estimation on the variety of work requirements in women's projects. Mostly these special requirements are called "the other" of women's work without giving exact definitions. To look for these definitions is very important for two reasons: To strengthen the professional understanding of the project workers and to publicise the quality and the difficulty of the tasks. Also we hope to gain some impact with-our findings on the ongoing discussion amongst project workers on the professionalisation of their work, the use and the limits of using professional tools and the political meaning of this change in the concept of women's self-help projects.
The data stem from about 20 independent women's projects in the Rhein-Main Metropolitan area from three different work fields: Shelters, counselling projects and educational projects. The methods used are participatory observation, qualitative interviews with experts and a time-budget analysis in each of the projects.

2. Setting boundaries and self-development when working In women's projects

Working with women in women's projects is often linked with a desire to do something for one's own well-being, in the sense of self-development and further development. What is often not realised - due to a simultaneous desire for closeness - is that self-discovery and self-development presuppose distancing oneself, recognising the otherness of the women one works with. A clinging to the idea of closeness is expressed, for example, in the belief of some colleagues that professional forms of help result in putting one's own interests before those of the other women, it being presupposed that one's own interests have a distancing character.

In the context of work on women's projects the question of setting boundaries is a particularly difficult one and awakens strong guilt feelings because of the fact that work with, and for, women is very close to the emotional reproduction generally done by women, and also close to motherliness (Bruckner 1992). Thus even professional women tend to distrust professionalism, giving preference to spontaneous help which is assumed to be closer to life's needs. As one young psychologist louts it In an interview:

"I am best when Ican be myself, just as I really am. Why do you need theories and methods, when instead you can simply go out among the people and help." (Rommelspacher, 1987:39).

Behind this attitude lies the notion that you only need to resort to methods and theories when you yourself are not "good". This attitude, however, does not exclude the possibility that work done in a more informal manner is often devalued as "just muddling through", and methods and theories secretly rated very highly, even overrated.

In the day to day work in women's project setting boundaries (not just between groups but also within them) is just as important* as closeness and caring consideration, both for the project workers and for the women and girls who come for help. It serves to create room for individual development. The ability to set boundaries, meaning letting the other woman go, being a model of independent womanhood, not a carbon copy of a clinging mother, this ability is something women have to learn from each other in the Course of their professional contacts. (see Flaake, 1989 and her comparable results with teachers). It requires a high level of acceptance of the other women and respect for her personal integrity. That is to say, the relationship between two women should not serve as an extension of oneself, should not have a purely mirroring function. The prerequisite for a genuine encounter, in the deepest sense of the term, is that women become aware of their differences, their diverging interests and needs, and that they do not just regret and lament this, but recognise its potential for their own individual self-development.

What tends to cause problems when dealing with other women is their inadequacies and weaknesses, which, when looked at more closely, often reflect one's own short-comings. A new aim In feminist work could be to stop ignoring these interconnections, which are well-known, but difficult to come to terms with. By recognising them, women could develop the capacity to estimate a measure of activity for themselves which is free of any Illusions of omnipotence or inadequacy.

Even though it may sound contradictory, one prerequisite for self-development is to set clear boundaries for oneself, and make a clear differentiation between one's own Ego and that of the other (see Ostner, 1986). Understood in this way, self-development can mean putting an end to otherwise never-ending responsibilities, it can be the cristallisatlon of what I can achieve and what I cannot. Progress along this path involves accepting one's own aggressive tendencies, one's own pretensions to power, one's own egoism, one's own need to be lazy, etc. These are emotions and strivings which for a long time women have simply not been allowed to have, and which, when they come to light, cause women anxiety. However, an acceptance of such forbidden strivings and their integration into one's own self-image could enable women to reach a more stable evaluation of their own person, in all its facets (see Lerner, 1990). This is something which has to be learned not only those women seeking help in better protecting themselves from male impositions. Active feminists, too, need to set an example.

In my view, this painful process towards separation cannot be avoided, not even shortened. Fear of independence is based on a usually unsuccessful or incomplete separation from the mother (see Chodorow, 1978; Benjamin, 1988). Cultural limitations to female individualisation are expressed not least in a continued attachment to the mother.

On the other hand, efforts made to avoid at all costs being emotionally overwhelmed by the pain suffered by other women are often the result not of secure ego-boundaries and professional considerations, but of an attempt to combat the wish for, and fear of, fusion with the other. What Is more important than battling with any feared rush of emotions, is to become aware of it, to feel it (as far as is possible). For in this counter-transference I can empathise with the feelings of the suffering person and react more appropriately. If these feelings are not allowed expression, it can happen that a project worker will press for a hurried solution just because she herself cannot bear the situation any longer and feels threatened by the "suction effect" of the unresolved problem. Not only can this result in pressure for hurried action, but also in a "lack of feeling", as all feelings now seem dangerous and have to be suppressed.

Any attempt to protect oneself from such a rush of feeling, for example by dealing with the problem more "methodically", is doomed to failure, as it amounts to nothing more than a superficial solution strategy. Methods are being instrumentalised just to keep the women or girls and their problems "at arm's length". Unavoidably, this limits the ability to emphathlse. Access to the unconscious patterns which form the basis of the other woman's suffering, however, Is only possible via the conscious experience of one's own reactions and the limits to what one can bear. If these become covered over by method, they cannot be experienced consciously and instead carve out a path for themselves unconsciously and uncontrolled. Used thus,

methods are not so much a helpful instrument as a shield against one's own anxiety. Of course, methods were also developed for this purpose (see Devereux, 1976), which makes it all the more important to examine why one should want to implement one at one given moment and in one particular way, rather than just availing of a method as an anchor in a storm. By instrumentalislng methods I construct a protective wall around me which does not primarily reflect an inner hardness, but more a stronghold against the threat of overwhelming emotions.
Another variation on this problematic theme of encountering other women is the form sometimes taken by what is intended as sympathy: I remain totally imprisoned in my own point of view, assuming as perfectly self-evident that it coincides with that of the other woman. After all, I "understand" her, and, because of our hypostatised similarity, I also know what is good for her.
A long-lasting scepticism towards all methodological work seems to be something very German. Method - often misunderstood as therapy - is equated with separation, and even more with imposing one's own will. Thus the fantasy is nourished that a non-methodological approach can function as a protection against imposing one's will. In the Netherlands I came across a greater acceptance of methodological work - understood as working In accordance with prescribed steps. A methodological approach offers not only a certain relief but also the possibility of a substitute activity, above and beyond one's own feelings, namely. At least this seems to be the unconscious expectation. Given their contrary defence structures, these two different approaches could throw some light on their respective blind spots. For this purpose, however, their respective understanding of the term method would have to be examined again closely.

3. Becoming aware of the hidden traps

Before going into the different approaches to using methods, as an expression of closeness and of distance, I feel it is necessary to recognise the dynamics underlying the projects so as to gain a deeper understanding of the problems ' involved. These dynamics are like traps which have been set along the path of the day to day project work and in which the project workers can get caught. The unconscious or preconscious "offers" emanating from the respective themes or project structures can be characterised as "traps". They influence professional behaviour more or less parallel, and even contrary, to the intended aim of the project. Thus they lead the way to the deep structures of the project. It is in the adequacies - and more often the inadequacies - of the project work that demands become obvious which are less conscious, or not conscious at all, but which still exist and exercise an effect.]:n analysing these deep structures, the question is not really what could be done better. There is often no concrete alternative available (for example, problems with the building in which the project is housed, or with a lack of staff or money). For this very reason it is important to pay attention to what unconscious effects these working conditions can have, how they can influence the whole atmosphere, not just

among the project workers but also among the clients. By taking these effects into account during the work, it is possible to avoid misunderstandings on all sides.
For this, it is necessary to get to know and understand not only the concrete and outward aspects of the work, but also those aspects which are covert, permeating the atmosphere "under cover" and influencing the work in an uncontrolled and unintended manner, It is these more secret aspects of the work which have to be brought out into the open so as to be able to integrate the constraints and wishes inherent in them into the work in as constructive a way as possible.
One example of such a trap is the overestimation of therapy as the only instrument which can "heal", by seeking out and finding that "inner point" which is the cause of all the suffering. One consequence of this over-rating of therapy is that discussion of concrete individual requirements and steps is -neglected and often even disregarded.
In the following I would like to illustrate some traps, In the sense of dilemmas, which turn up in those women's projects which have to do with violence towards women. These dilemmas became evident in the course of our research work being done currently at the Fachhochschule Frankfurt (Our thanks are due to the women working in the respective projects examined.)

Dilemma 1: Themes carve a path for themselves.

For example in projects aimed at helping sexually abused women and girls, and which guarantee them counselling, a bed for the night, and optional activities. In these projects the theme of setting boundaries, of dealing with intrusions, plays an important role, not just as a concrete problem experienced by the women and girls, but also one reflected in the project structures. Let me give an illustration of this:
One of the refugees tries to protect itself and the survivors of sexual abuse from instrusions by means of massive security measures at the entrance. On the other hand, fathers and teachers (male and female) are allowed into the project rooms, even though the project workers occasionally have the feeling of being "used" by them. That is to say, they allow access to persons who have more or less acquired it by insistence, but who are not the people the project workers really want to have around them. Once, when it was too late, they noticed that a man had left their private toilet dirty. This awakened the feeling that they had somehow been '"dirtied". This is a feeling which in fact many of their clients also have in the context of their experience with violence and sexual abuse. This act of dirtying the toilet, which is experienced as a massive instrusion, is referred to repeatedly, related as It is to the very theme of the project. Violence and sexual abuse offend boundaries, break limits. Even the project workers feel they have been taken unaware on their own premises by this act. The lock on the door, therefore, is really useless and does not guarantee real protection.
A further illustration:

The behaviour of the project women towards the observer from the research group also hints at the difficulty of boundaries: The observer is said to be "breathing down their necks". At the same time, they too behave towards her in a manner which is repeatedly "intrusive": this they do by hindering her In her work, trying to draw her into their project by relating dreadful stories from their day to day project work. On the one hand no one should come too close to them (breathe down their neck), on the other, everyone should get involved in the project (drawn in by the suction effect).

These dynamics also apply in the interaction with some of the clients, especially with those women or girls who are felt to be too insistent, expecting a counselling appointment as soon as possible, though for no really Justified reason, as it often turns out later. The project workers give in and then feel they have been "tricked". Certain clients are not doubt insistent, but it is the project worker's problem If she cannot resist this and has nothing at her disposal with which to combat It and withstand the so-called suction effect. Thus the inescapable and all-pervasive problem of abuse of boundaries, sexual and otherwise, Is experienced again within the project at different levels. The project workers sense this and feel obliged to react accordingly. Each woman coming for held is presented with a totally "unsullied" situation: the project women clean up any "signs" of the women who went before, in an attempt to break through the vicious circle (quite irrespective of the fact that at a rational level tidying up makes sense). The children's room - also used as a waiting room and for counselling - is cleaned up for a girl who comes for counselling directly after her sister. Thus, unconsciously, this waiting room is treated like the emotionally charged toilet. The assumption being in both cases that intrusions can take place, leaving "marks" which then have to be cleaned up by the project workers. The latter feel helpless in this situation. One result of all this is a permanent emotional pendulum, swinging to and fro from a feeling of being intruded upon to a need to try and set up boundaries.

With regard to sexual abuse, the danger of being drawn In to the sphere of transgression so strong that attempts to set boundaries or limits may sometimes even seem arbitrary. For example, some projects have rigid rules as regards when and how long they can be reached by phone, and in some there is great secrecy about which tasks a trainee is allowed to do and which not. This struggle to set boundaries is in no way just a reflection of the competence of the workers, it is a component of the actual theme of sexual abuse itself. The same struggle to set boundaries is also reflected in the counselling itself, and in how the life stories of the women and girl clients are dealt with.

The consequence to be drawn from all this should not be to avoid the issue from the very beginning, which I feel is impossible anyway, but to become aware of the "suction power" of the theme, and to reflect upon it on the basis of one's own emotional reactions. In this way the capacity to empathise with the fate of the abused women and girls can be maintained and be given a solid basis.

Sexuality, an equally central, and mostly unconscious, theme In women's refuges,

also has its effects on the work done there. I would again like to illustrate this:
In the large workroom of one women's refuge - a room used as a meeting place for project workers and inhabitants alike, both for professional and private reasons - it soon became evident that sexuality was "In the air" during a relaxed, casual discussion. On that occasion the observer from the research group was reminded of the atmosphere in an "open house", where mixed activities also take place (although consciously intended in the refuge is the mixture of private and professional). The observer herself was discussing the book "The Tin Drum" by Gunther Grass with one of the project workers. In this novel a somewhat coarse form of (hetero)-sexuality plays a central role. The observer found this open-house atmosphere (the open doors, the relaxed mood) quite pleasant. The workers were available for a chat, and contacts with the women living in the refuge were good.
The associations "open house", "mixed activities" and "The Tin Drum" are sexual. Why? In women's refuges in particular the opposition open/closed is of central importance: the house is open to all women but closed to the outside world (in many refuges the windows on the ground floor are barred). Women are supposed to find shelter and protection here. Men are to be kept outside. One of the reasons for these measures is after all sexuality, that Is to say, sexual relations between men and women which had become violent. The theme of sexuality is present In these refuges whether one likes it or not, whether it goes noticed or unnoticed, and In many different ways. The women living there usually wanted to have sexual relations with men, and still do.
Not all of them, therefore, are enthusiastic about the fact that men are excluded. So men and sexuality are present, although "kept outside". When sex with men is prohibited or taboo, then It tends to take place "under the skirts" as in "The Tin Drum". (The father of the book's hero is conceived outdoors, in public, under the wide skirts of his grandmother, where she had hidden him from the police.) In Grass' book sexual events are often described in a slightly coarse way. Sex is not always pleasant, thus corresponding to the experience of the women living in the refuge, whose sexual experiences were not always, or very seldom pleasant. But sex is still none the less attractive. In the refuge some of the women are "wild" about men, something which is diametrically opposed to the usual notions the outside public have of what the women In such houses are like.
As only women live in the refuges, sex is only possible with women, regardless of their respective orientation. Sex is presented in the house and even locked in. Within the women's movement and in many women's refuges love among women has been propagated as the preferable alternative to heterosexual love. ("Feminism Is the theory, lesbianism the practice".) Today this is less openly the case, but that does not mean that the topic has been "dealt with". At most it has been put out of the way. In whatever way the different refuges decide to deal with the question of sex, it still remains a topic, and a very controversial one at that. Some of the women are looking for a man, even if he is not allowed into the house. The project workers themselves are usually more reserved towards men, especially towards the kind

of men these women look for and very easily find. Is this constellation experienced by some of the women as a repeat of the mother's prohibition about sex? How do women experience being '"locked in" among other women, and the "openness'" which is prevalent there? How do the project workers react to the women who are "wild" about men? Whatever way these questions are 'answered in the individual cases, in all the refuges the theme of sex and eroticism between men and women, and between women and. women, plays a significant role. And this theme, whether dealt with openly or covertly, carves out a path for itself and is a cause of jealousy, competition and contempt.

The husbands of the women living In the refuges have broken limits, overstepped boundaries. But perhaps it is self-deception to expect that women are incapable of breaking limits (sexual and otherwise). Thus protection for the women in the refuge is also limited, and this is something which the inhabitants (and even the workers), perhaps fear unconsciously, so it should be thematised in the course of the work.

Dilemma 2: Never-ending responsibilities: a wish or an imposition, but one that results in discontinuity

Sometimes writing the minutes of a meeting, filling out expense sheets, or finishing a report takes a very long time (maybe a whole day). This is due to the many and varied interruptions common in a women's refuge. Some typical interruptions are: telephone calls, short conversations with or inquiries from other colleagues, tasks dealt with "in between" which seem urgent or just happen to come to mind, a woman wants something (keys, counters for the washing machine etc.). These interruptions are experienced as annoying but are also considered to be essentially normal or Inalterable. They result from the given living and working conditions In the refuge (shared offices, everyone Involved In every task, so as to exclude no one), and also from an acceptance that everything is of equal importance and urgency. This widespread attitude to project work "arises" from the type of work to be done, from the colourful diversity of the task, to which one just succumbs.

Special effort is required if one is to resist this and try and set up clear working structures. If this is done, however, the work then takes on a different character, based more on separation and division than on allroundness, simultaneity and inter-connectedness. The un-structured approach to project work seems to appeal to many women, even though they suffer under the pressure of having to do everything at once. But a certain fascination seems to emanate from the demand to keep a clear head in the chaos, to manage to pull off something by yourself and yet still be part of a whole. Is it possible that, symbolically speaking, mother's hands have some bearing on this; the hands that never rest and possibly even exert power, making further Investigation into the work process seem superfluous, even immoral? Nevertheless, the question is how to preserve some of the advantages of this allround approach to work, without Incurring the same measure of frustration and inefficiency caused by so much additional work and the never-ending responsibility.

But first an example of the dilemma from the perspective of a project worker: "There is the problem that you want to be In on all the tasks, so you have to keep everything in your head, and the pressure Is just enormous, because it just does not work.

If someone were to say, two women do the administration work and the others don't have to. Or two women organise the event together, and the others need not worry about it. It would be better If things were like that more often. Because things tend to get overlooked, or the unpleasant tasks are avoided. And the women living in the refuge, they can sometimes almost swallow you up if they want. So it Is important to learn to set limits and to say when you have had enough. But you know, a women's refuge Is a great place for practice." (Unpublished interview from the current research being done at the Fachhochschule, Frankfurt)

In the meantime women's projects have abandoned the Idea of '"everyone being responsible for everything, everyone being able to do everything equally well". Forms for the division of labour have been found, but these efforts are often undermined in practice in the day to day work, particularly in women's refuges with their hundreds of simultaneous demands. I think the reason for this is that in this particular kind of women's project "all kinds of tasks possible" turn up and generally have to do with the survival of the inhabitants and the survival of the project. Thus the subjective wish to be responsible for everything and capable of everything is nurtured here, a wish which is inherent in traditionally female work. Furthermore, this approach to the work satisfies a need on the part of the workers to be identified with the whole project and not "relegated" to just one particular task where you quickly lose sight of the whole project, and instead of being involved in a totally new "kind of work", are just doing a normal professional job, with all the dangers of becoming estranged from the project. Behind this is the fantasy that in feminist women's projects there is no room for competition and you are protected from isolation and ostracisation.

But immanent in this approach Is the threat of being overwhelmed by the flood of tasks to be done. In order to protect themselves against this, project workers often make efforts to "create order", for example by insisting that appointed times are kept to.]:n the face of the difficulty of finding inner and outer forms for this desire for order, decisions made in this regard are not always in accordance with rational criteria. They often apply to a relatively unsuitable object, for example, to the children in the refuge. They are then trained, unconsciously, on behalf of all the others in the house, to be absolutely punctual, even though this means that they have to rush wildly around the house. But then perhaps this is part of the decision: given that so much is against strict structures In a refuge, they can only be imposed when everyone has to suffer - in this case from the noise the children make. Everyone is involved and not Just those directly effected by the imposition of punctuality: the workers nerves are on edge; the children have to put up with their edginess.

This example shows how important it is to give some thought to when and where efforts are suddenly made to impose order, and what the emotional reactions behind these measures are. Perhaps the children were chosen because it is easier to impose rules on them. There is no denying that for children punctuality and regularity are important, but given the project as a whole, this measure has something compulsive about it. It arises from an Inner difficulty to create structures at all, to say nothing of maintaining and imposing them. This problem is particularly great in women's refuges where the proximity of work and life is most evident. In my opinion, projects which try and solve this problem by believing that they can bring all the tasks into line with a concrete established structure and XXXX methods ignore the specific demands of women's refuges. What we need is to find a compromise between structures more typical of a children's home, and a total lack of structure. This should be a compromise with which the project workers (and of course the refuge women) can come to terms with, i.e. one which corresponds to their way of working and at the same time serves their purpose.

These dilemmas, presented as traps inherent in the work involved in women's projects, are all variations on the central theme of creating boundaries or setting limits, and the tension which exists between the expectation of closeness and the necessity for distance. Only a clarification of the related emotional and structural uncertainties can in the long run guarantee a solid basis for continued caring and supportive work. It is indispensable for feminist project workers to confront themselves with this theme.

A thorough discussion of dilemmas - like the ones mentioned above could form a basis on which the use of methods, their possibilities and their limits in the specific project and work field are to be decided upon.

3.3 A Dutch Teacher of Social Work in Frankfurt and Erfurt

Robert Ploem

ABSTRACT
International teachers' exchange is a relatively new phenomenon in European Social Work Education, and in the history of the School of Social Work of the Hogeschool van Amsterdam it is unique. In 1992 our school in Amsterdam welcomed a visiting lecturer from the School of Social Work of the Fachhochschule (Higher Vocational College) of Frankfurt am Main in Germany. The School of Social Work (Fachbereich Sozialwesen) of the Fachhochschule Erfurt (in the Eastern German state of Thuringia) invited me to be a visiting lecturer from the Netherlands. I also taught in January, 1992 and 1993, in the 'Fortbildung' (an educational week during the final, practical year) at the Frankfurt School of Social Work. The experiences of the teachers and evaluations by students are reviewed and a model and procedure for future exchanges is proposed.

I. INTRODUCTION

In 1988, the School of Social Work of the Hogeschool van Amsterdam (Higher Vocational College) began organising small teachers' colloquia in co-operation with several Faculties of Social Work in Germany and one in England. This resulted in a pioneer conference in Amsterdam in April, 1989, where educators had the chance to exchange experiences in teaching and supervision, compare curricula and talk about developments in the field.

At the second colloquium in Manchester in 1991, I initiated a meeting to explore the possibilities of teachers' exchange. Back in the Netherlands I became chairman of our faculty's International Affairs Project, and I conducted a small survey among schools we were acquainted with in Germany and the United Kingdom to look for exchange candidates. I was also encouraged by Joop van Scheijndel of the Head Office of the Hogeschool van Amsterdam to seek candidates who might be interested in becoming a visiting lecturer in our school in the spring of 1992. We learned that the Dutch ST 11 programme, a government scheme to stimulate international relations in education, provides for partial funding of visiting lecturers. These efforts resulted in a visiting lectureship for Margrit Brückner of the Fachhochschule Frankfurt.

Around this time I met a colleague friend Dr. Joachim Wieler at the European Regional Group Conference of the International Association of Schools of Social Work (IASSW) in Spa, Belgium. He turned out to be working at the newly-rounded School of Social Work in Erfurt, Thuringia, one of the so-called 'New Länder' in Germany. He invited me to become a guest teacher there for a month in 1992. I was also invited by the Frankfurt School of Social Work to teach in the 'Fortbildung', an week of instruction forming part of the students' fourth, practical training year.

II. VISITING LECTURER AT THE HOGESCHOOL VAN AMSTERDAM

Shortly after I became international affairs co-ordinator in our faculty, we decided to apply for the funding of a visiting lecturer in the spring of 1992. Everything had to be arranged on short notice to meet the final application deadline, but thanks to the co-operation of our Faculty Director, Kete Kervezee, we succeeded in organising a trial visiting lectureship. We chose Dr. Margrit Brückner of the Fachhochschule Frankfurt — who had replied to my questionnaire — because she teaches on women's issues, one of our school's target areas for special attention. Her fluency in English formed another advantage. We applied for and obtained STIR funding for this project, which meant some 4000 guilders compensation for the Frankfurt School of Social Work and 1100 guilders for housing her in Amsterdam. I was very lucky to find five weeks' furnished accommodation for that price. She was assigned to the Part-Time Social Work programme and I began recruiting students who could speak either English or German and who were interested in one of the two seminars she offered.

We had little experience at recruiting students from the other degree courses in our faculty (cultural and societal education and socio-pedagogic aid) for our seminars, and none at all in offering a seminar given in a foreign language. While our students must speak one foreign language, this is not necessarily English: it may be Turkish, Moroccan, or any other language, in order to facilitate admission of students from ethnic minority groups. Dutch university students, by contrast, must have a reading knowledge of English.

One of the difficulties we had to overcome was that there was no tradition of elective course elements in the part-time programmes: all elements were required. this meant I had to negotiate with the various teams for permission to substitute this seminar for another.

By the time Dr. Brückner arrived, I had recruited two groups of female students, a total of 15. Some of them attended both seminars. The seminars were very well received by the students and were positively evaluated at their close. Dr. Brückner also visited a number of institutions in the field and lectured twice to our staff. As we were involved in a merger at the time, only a small number of staff members attended these lectures. Dr. Brückner still collaborates today with our faculty group on women's studies, and our faculty uses materials provided by her in women's studies seminars and in student exchange orientation. Besides the exchange on women's studies there is an exchange scheme for first-year students. About 20 Frankfurt and 20 Amsterdam students took part in these one-week programmes this academic year.

Evaluation

As an initial project in our faculty, we may call it a success. Both students and teachers expressed satisfaction with the programmes, and contacts with a number of staff 'members have been intensified.

What I learned from this project:

- colleagues must be included in the informing, motivating and recruiting of students for exchange programmes
- our school needs to select and stimulate teachers in the various branches of
- study who are willing to introduce visiting lecturers' subjects into their own instruction
- the visiting lecturer should receive guidance from a local colleague or administrato
- it should be Clear how many credits students can earn with the seminars offered
- it is not easy to find affordable housing.
- Clear arrangements have to be made with the college for paying the visiting lecturers (it took over Seven months for Dr. Brückner to get her money).

III. AN AMSTERDAMER ABROAD

In the summer of 1988 I visited an international conference on social work education for the first time: the World Congress of the IASSW in Vienna. This experience gave me the courage to write a contribution for the European Regional Group Conference in Bled, Slovenia, in the fall of 1989. As a result of my paper on the integration of socialisation differences into the teaching of social work students (Ploem, 1991), I was invited to fulfil visiting lectureships in German social work schools at Frankfurt am Main and Erfurt, and to lecture to teachers at the West London Institute of Higher Education and at the Sociale Hogeschool in Ghent, Belgium.

An Amsterdamer in Frankfurt

Dr. Margrit Brückner of the School of Social Work (Fachbereich Sozialarbeit) invited me to Frankfurt in January, 1992, to lecture for a week during the so-called 'Praktikantenbildung', a programme of further education for social work trainees. In Frankfurt students obtain their diploma after three years' study, but to qualify as a social worker they must complete an additional practical training year within three more years. In the course of that year they return to college a few times for a week of instruction. While fulfilling their traineeships they earn half to three quarters of a social worker's salary!

On Monday morning about a hundred such students gathered in the auditorium and received more information on the five programmes being offered. They had been sent preliminary information beforehand. My main topic was working on different social identities of one's own: gender or sex identity, social class of parents, being German and being a social worker.

Around thirty-five students, about one third of the practical year, chose my course. As I had prepared myself for a training group of 10 to 12 students, this meant I had to reorganise my seminar. I had to give up my idea of tutoring. I lectured on the subjects and had students reflect on them in small groups, reporting back later. After two days I put four questions to them to help evaluate what had been done so far. The questions were:

- What have you learned so far about the topics, about yourself and about being a social worker?
- What did you like about the lecturer and the other students?
- Are there specific topics you want to explore further?
- What should be changed in the course: organisation, lecturer's behaviour, other students' behaviour?

The overall reactions of the students were very positive: most of them could formulate concrete remarks about what they had learned on some topics. They also indicated subjects they would like to go into more deeply, and that gave me the chance to adjust my programme. Most of the students were satisfied with the way we were working together. Some preferred to work longer in the small groups, some wished more in-depth discussion in the larger group.

In the closing evaluation, most students said they found the session on their identification with the social work profession surprising and stimulating. In the beginning quite a few had said they 'did not want to be a social worker' — which would seem problematic at the least for people 3 to 6 months from qualifying as social workers! They said they suffered a lot from negative images within German society of "Sozialarbeit" and from the relatively low status accorded to the profession. We worked hard on creating their own *positive image of the social worker* which they could willingly represent. They were quite surprised to discover that they themselves could begin redefining the image of the social worker into an idea of a proud social worker.

I found that the students in general

- were quite adept at the theoretical, critical level
- were very much concerned about the people they worked with
- were good at carrying on discussions
- differed in their experience with self-reflection from very much to very little
- have experienced quite divergent styles of tutoring, from very personal to very political.

On the other hand I found that

- exploring their own social identities was new for most students
- many students could not define the domain of 'Sozialarbeit' and found it hard to define their own social work methods
- most had difficulty coping with the negative image social workers have in Germany.

Some remarks at the organisational level:

- Meetings with department heads etc. should be arranged in advance, and the same goes for visits to field institutions.

- The status of the programme being offered and the available credits should be made clear to lecturers and students.
- Payment should be prompter (I got paid six months later).

Frankfurt revisited

This year I again went to teach in Frankfurt. This time I brought German language study materials to support my teaching. Drawing on the experiences I had meanwhile had in Erfurt the year before (see below), I added another social identity: 'What does it mean to be a German or be seen as a German'. One group of six students went into this subject more deeply: they found it very hard to identify as a German; some hardly dared to leave their country nowadays. We talked about possibilities of identifying as a European, a world citizen, or a more regional citizen instead. We discussed how to cope with being discriminated against as a German while travelling.
The students' evaluation was again very positive and stimulating. I will be back in Frankfurt.

An Amsterdamer in Erfurt

At the Spa European Regional Group Conference of the IASSW in 1991 I ran into Prof. Dr. Joachim Wieler Loewen, who had attended the first Colloquium in Amsterdam four years ago as a lecturer from the Darmstadt School of Social Work. He turned out to be working in the newly rounded school of social work in Erfurt, Thuringia, one of Germany's Eastern states, and invited me to become a visiting teacher at their school.
We agreed I would come for one month in June, 1992, and teach on social identities and Social work with migrants. I was to live, as my colleagues did, in the former communist party school in an odd little room with basic facilities. Although I had limited to 20 the number of students for each seminar, 25 signed up for one and 24 for the other. I was pleased to discover that some of the books I use in my Amsterdam teaching had been translated into German. I made a selection from these materials, drew up an accompanying study guide, and had 50 copies made in Amsterdam.
In the late spring of 1992, my partner and I went by car with some basics - two boxes of books, a ghetto blaster with twenty compact discs, pots and pans etc. - and I made myself at home in this room. Let us now look at my experiences in more detail.

a. Terms of the visiting lectureship

The post was made possible by the special programme for the new German states set up within the European Community's Erasmus Programme. In preliminary correspondence with Prof. Dr. Joachim Wieler Loewen of the Fachhochschule Erfurt, 1 had agreed to offer a weekly four-hour seminar on two subjects: 'Social psychology: social identities, German identities, identities of social strata, cultural identities, identity as a social worker' and 'Social work with migrant men and women'. I was also to lead a two-day seminar for training supervisors, persons who provide guidance to the trainees on the job, entitled 'Aspects of practical training supervision'. Enrolment in each group was to be limited to 20.

b. How the work progressed

Two months in advance of enrolment, students and training supervisors were furnished with a brief summary of the contents of the seminars.

The seminars proceeded as announced. Participants were given teaching materials which included a study guide stating goals and planning and a selection of text materials.

Although about 25 students had registered for each seminar, only 8 turned up for the first sessions. After a faculty meeting had consented to allow the seminar to count for degree credit, attendance rose to about 20 from the second week onwards. In the seminar for training supervisors, only 10 of the 20 persons who enrolled took part.

The students showed great interest in the instruction. They participated with enthusiasm, studied the topics and reading materials intensely, contributed their own examples and experiences, and critically analysed the theories dealt with. Discussing the identities of the Eastern German regions in relation to the Western ones proved especially provocative. For this we used parts of a book entitled D/e *Einheit beginnt zu zweit. Ein deutsch-deutsches Zwiegespräch (Unity* Starts with Two People. A German-to-German Conversation) by Michael Lukas Moeller and Hans-Joachim Maaz. We examined which parts of these identities are important and lasting, and we discovered how important it is to incorporate these elements into the new, greater Germany. Elements of the past such as the East German secret police, the *Stasi,* were also dealt with, using a Dutch television interview with Andreas Sinakowski, an East German defector and author of the book *Das Verhör (The* Interrogation).

Students said they especially valued the clear structure of the seminars. Both their evaluations and their final written exams revealed how intensely and productively they were involved in the subject matter dealt with.

The seminars for training supervisors served two purposes: to provide information on the theory and practice of supervision, and to exchange experiences among the supervisors themselves. As most supervisors were not social workers themselves, the issue of the professional image of social workers came to play an important part in the discussions. Aspects of the 'German identities' also repeatedly came up during the sessions. The supervisors tackled the subjects with interest, and they experienced them as useful and supportive to their work in the current situation of radical change within the social work profession. The study materials were also judged beneficial. A faculty official was present at the dosing session to provide the faculty with impulses from social work practice.

c. evaluation and conclusions

I feel I succeeded during my visiting lectureship in getting my information across to the students, and in confronting them with Dutch views and standpoints as well as with unfamiliar, 'foreign' working methods. Debate with a Dutch lecturer proved especially useful when it came to questions of German identities. Contrary to my initial fears, communication between me and the students and trainees from the former East Germany presented no problems. Encounters with faculty colleagues were possible only to a limited extent, because faculty meetings were scheduled parallel to my seminars and many colleagues left Erfurt on Thursday evenings. Looking back, I also regret that so little contact developed with social workers.

For future visiting lectureships, I suggested considering the following points:

- better integration of the visiting lecturer's seminars into the curriculum
- a closer fit between subject matter dealt with by the visiting lecturer and that of the corresponding local faculty member
- increased collaboration between local faculty members and visiting lecturers -
- arranging visits for visiting lecturers to institutions in the field, if possible pri or to the start of their teaching duties
- for more effective organisation, the visiting lecturer should be enabled to visit the college personally well in advance of the visiting lectureship

IV. GUIDELINES FOR TEACHERS' EXCHANGE

On the basis of my experiences with international teachers' exchange, I have drawn up a list of points that need attention from people who are organising such exchanges:

Preparations

Begin by doing the following:

determine where your department's expertise lies

- decide which subjects your school may need expert knowledge on
- find out which college manager (administrator) might be interested in teachers' exchange
- find out whether your school has its own international affairs policy and budget
- inquire which lecturers have the appropriate expertise and may be interested in either being sent out or working with the visiting lecturer
- find out what funding programmes exist in your own country, which European funds may be available, and whether there are cultural agreements with the country your department wants to enter into exchange relations with

- determine the subject(s) you would like to see dealt with and recruit the lecturers who are willing to work with the visiting lecturer
- select and invite the visiting lecturer
- apply for the funds
- determine how many credits students will be offered, and distribute leaflets
- outlining the visiting lecturer's proposals
- announce a date for an informatory meeting with students (and staff)

Realisation

After finding support and money, take the following steps:

- invite the chosen lecturer to your school for 'an orientation visit, and ask them to bring more detailed teaching proposals and, if possible, whatever written, video and other materials they will use
- decide on the subjects, the number of teaching hours and credits, and the type of students that will be interested in the material
- make arrangements for additional lecturing to staff members and / or field workers
- set goals and draw up criteria for evaluating the teaching and for gauging the benefits to the school, teachers' collaboration, and the curriculum
- introduce the visiting teacher to all colleagues and to the director or head of de partment
- try to schedule the information session with the potential students during this period
- make arrangements with visiting lecturer and the administration about payments, travel allowance, housing costs etc.
- set three to four fixed hours in the week at which the visiting lecturer and staff members will be free and could work together during the stay
- make arrangements for any field visits
- look for and rent appropriate housing
- find the lecturer a room and a desk in the school

Execution

- announce the lectures and seminars on time to teachers and students in your own school (and to social workers in the field)
- publicise the subjects to be offered and recruit interested students
- inform the visiting lecturer of the schedules of co-operating teachers
- introduce the visiting lecturer to teaching staff, managers and supporting staff
- make arrangements for photocopying, telephone etc.
- schedule a final evaluation session for the students
- organise a meeting between the lecturers who co-operated, the visiting lecturer and the manager(s)
- organise an overall evaluation of the visiting lectureship and make arrangements about who reports to whom and in what form.

3.4 The Intensive Workshop - an innovative Course in cooperative Teaching and Learning transnational Aspects of Social Work

M. Widmark-Nilsson

People are different, groups are different, students are different, teachers are different... this truism is the lasting impression we have from our weeks of teaching and learning between the Schools of Social Work in Frankfurt and Stockholm in the years of 1990, 1991 and 1992.
The co-operation between the two schools started - as it almost always does - with personal contact between teachers from the two schools, and after a "planning trip" to Frankfurt and meeting with deans and teachers involved, we from Stockholm decided to agree to the German initiative and try to build up an exchange programme for the two schools.
We agreed upon the following: Each year in May ten students and two teachers from the respective schools meet during one week for a common study programme. We found that it could be useful to use a family case as a starting point, and discuss it from different perspectives. The family system is something that most social workers have experience of working with in some respect or other. This would create a framework for understanding similarities and differences in the German and Swedish context.
In keeping with this view, we clarified the following goals and content for the intensive programme...

Principle objectives of the study programme

The structure of the workshop should contribute to a more *dense experience* in cooperation compared to what ordinary types of didactics in higher education can provide. Why did we choose such an unusual approach?
In Social Work the perhaps most effective instrument for change is the relationship between client and social worker.
The training of that dimension is a task of greatest importance. The kind of meeting offered in a lecture is not sufficient to cope with this need.
In this programme we wanted to create a variety of important encounters cross nationality borders. Having to meet in different contexts without escape as a possibility and to reflect and give and take feedback on the experiences, we thought might be highly productive.

How to implement this?
In working together *managing everyday life* (organise cooking, cleaning and leisure time activities together e.g.) the students and teachers would have to learn to cope with the needs and demands of two nationally different groups.

The experience of *direct confrontation* with different habits and prejudices would, we hoped, give opportunity to unforeseen situations. Working with these situations should increase competence in the process of creating a good relationship and contribute to a further mutual understanding. Scheduled working hours should definitely prioritise *group work practice* to formal lectures/lessons.

Content of the Workshops

We wanted the content of the intensive programme to contribute to the following goals:

* to find a possibility for students and teachers to become *more familiar with a foreign welfare system*(with a focus on social work with families).
* to train and encourage the skills of the workshop-members to *compare and analyse* transnational aimes and concepts; skills that seem to be more relevant every year with European development.
* to make different aspects of the respective group's *own welfare system more visible* in education. In the mirror of other ways of thinking, you learn more of your own identity.
* to create an unique opportunity to *let "old" learnings and experiences come forward.* The students have to look back in their college years for material. The use and presentation of this material should be an integrative experience for some parts of their education.

Further more: The process of this intensive weekly workshop was expected to stimulate every student's own creativity. To prepare, present and discuss various topics together with foreign students must be an useful experience.

Why "Working With Families"?

The key title of the intensive program has since the start been:
"Working with families". Why? This theme could be the arena where a lot of ends meet. The family, as a phenomenon, is of great interest. Here we have one of the meeting points between society and individual. Here we also can try to understand relations between private life and public life.
What ideas and beliefs a country accords to "the family", must tell a lot about that country in general. How do politics, social policies and legislation influence and shape "the family"? What rights and obligations do "the family" have? How can a family exist, and under what conditions?
Of special interest is to compare how social workers conceptualise "the family". Are families the context within which we organise help when needed by the individual? What ideologies lead us in this work? What theories and methods do we use?

Structure of guidelines

The guidelines for the three workshops had similarities, although they have had a different evolution. You can roughly find three parts where the comparative perspective has been used.

1) The presentation of frameworks for social work with families in the respective countries

Some knowledge of the welfare system has seemed important to begin with.
Social policy, legislation, and beliefs of ordinary people and professionals are structures that in many ways determine practice for the social worker.
A couple of short lectures given by teachers, followed by discussions, have been offered.
Some comparative reflections found in the workshops:
***German conditions:** Family is a stronger institution. Marriage is more important. The society shouldn't intervene in normal cases or minor problem. The family itself should take care of the family members. If necessary.: social services should support and help the family - family preservation is a primary goal.*
***Swedish conditions**: Public service more often take over some of the family s rights and duties. Individuals (especially children) are objects for help and support. When family-based services are provided, they are more seen as a specific method of treatment.*

2) The presentation of social work practice with families

In this second part we have met with examples of social work in the field.
Different methods and practices have been presented by both students and teachers. The workshops have also involved at least one day for study visits, where we have visited services that work with families in trouble.

All these presentations have lead to interesting comparative discussions.
Some questions that we have touched:
* Who are the clients in respective countries? Is the client-population in the proces of changing? How come?
* Why and how do they come in contact with social workers?
* What kind of organisation / activities do we have to meet the clients and their needs?

Some further reflections found in the workshops:
There seems to be a big difference in employers/commission givers:
***Swedish social work** is generally organised by society. The municipality, the county and the state provides for at least 90 % of all activities.*

***German social work** seem to be built on other grounds. A lot of initiatives are made possible by voluntary organisations. The big churches have for instance organisations that employ many social workers.*

3) Application of new and old knowledge on cases

How to handle a case like this in our country? Different approaches are obvious when comparing!
Perhaps this has been the most appreciated part of the three courses. The students have found it very useful and enjoyable to work together in their groups with a case unknown to them all.
It has been most challenging for the students to present their own ideas about working with such a case to another nationality.
Some final reflections found in the workshops:
*Does **German social work** have to be more inventive and creative? German social workers seem to have to work harder to create possibilities and find resources to meet their clients needs. Perhaps there are not so many 'fixed" structures to lean on.The **Swedish system** seems to have more "wealth". It also seems to be more institutionalized and organized (too much?). A certain problem should be taken care of in a setting planned for that problem, and there are many settings*

EVALUATION OF THE WORKSHOPS

Regarding the principle objective of the workshop(i.e. the dense experiences in co-operation and didactics) we have come to the following conclusions:
We think we have managed to create a setting as dense as we wanted. We have lived together in remote areas, in plain accomodations. We have taken care of our daily needs by cooking etc. together. Most activities we have done together, and there has been different opinions on how to spend the spare time. We have been able to discuss and find compromises. This process has fulfilled our expectations. We do have created a lot of interesting, challenging encounters.
What we still need to develop is a better way to benefit from these situations by reflecting and discussing the cause of events. We have to create more opportunities in the study programme for feedback and evaluation.
We find that we have implemented group work-oriented methods in our pedagogy, but we still find that it is desirable to increase opportunities for nationally mixed groups. We also have to reflect upon how to ameliorate the quality of every group work-practice. Stimulating the students and the teachers to take on challenging topics in an inviting and spirited climate will be next step.
The students evaluations of these workshops have been very positive on the whole. Some have even regarded this experience as a highlight in their education. Of course the students also have recognised deficiencies in structure and content. Thus

they have contributed to the improvement of the programme. A few have complained about things like: to much time spent for cooking, to authoritarian decision-making according to leisure time, to primitive accommodation etc.

What happened during the three years?

In order to give you a glimpse of what kind of interactions we have found "really" went on, here are our narratives ...

The first time, the week was spent in a little village called Wirberg. The Swedish group, all female, arrived by train in Frankfurt, rented two cars and managed to find their way to the meeting place in the hectic German traffic jam - this could only be a stressful experience for the more rural Swedes! But the house was beautifully situated and the weather on the whole favourable. The teachers had not met before, and we have a feeling that the German male teachers found the Swedish teachers to be strong women (and strong they are). The Swedish teachers seemed to have decided to carry through their special agenda and pedagogy and the German teachers thought afterwards that they accepted it too readily. There where different opinions on how to spend the leisure time in the evenings, some in the groups wanted to stay up socialising late, while others were disturbed by music and noise.

This is an example of what can happen when you have not had, or given yourself opportunity to talk through the conditions under which you are going to co-operate. The students however gave a positive response to the programme, made friends and kept in contact long after their week together.

The original German group came together and met with a new group of Swedish students and teachers in May 1991. We Swedes had rented a house in the Stockholm archipelago on an island called Barnens Ö (Children's Island). The change in the group formation was a result of the need to accommodate the differences in our respective study programmes. The Germans with their project-oriented educational methods, keep the classes together for a longer time, if we have got it right.

Our Swedish students have studies almost five semesters before they can choose this intense course, the Germans only one year the first time we meet, and two the next time. This highlights our joint need to accommodate differences. On the other hand the German students are much better prepared when it comes to comprehension of different European welfare systems, including the Swedish one. The capacity to speak English was better in the Swedish group but this difference has narrowed in recent years. The atmosphere among the students in this context was, as we see it, very good, open-minded with an urge to learn from each other without being competitive. The setting was also favourable: a big house with space for different activities; people could stay up nights if they liked without disturbing others who would-like to sleep. The nature and the closeness to the sea - and the bright summer nights invited the participants to outdoor activities. The composition of the Swedish group was also different from the year before; more mature students we would say, willing to take more responsibility. On the whole we had an impression

that the week together was a successful experience for students as well as teachers. Back to Wirberg again in May 1992 there were two new groups to meet and again a different composition of people.
While the teachers were the same as previous year in Sweden, few in the Swedish group knew each other previously. This meant they liked to spend some time to get to know each other, with the result that they did not socialise so much with their German peers. They also found, at least some of them, the cooking too time-consuming and did not take the same responsibility as the German students did. Again we found the house too small. We think we all recognise the need for space in this type of meetings. Luckily the weather was marvellous so we could spend a lot of the time outdoors. The case study seen from different perspectives was appreciated as usual, as well as the study visits into Frankfurt, not forgetting the reception by the Mayor in Laubach and the night spent in the old town, quite an experience for Swedes not spoiled with many old historical sites!

A Trinational Programme - a few words about the fourth Workshop

After we presented this paper at the Frankfurt Colloquium in April 1993 one more workshop has taken place in Sweden in May *1993*. Now a third partner, students and teachers from Hogeschool van Amsterdam, joined us.
Did some evident change appear in the structure or performance of the workshop? Although we kept the original idea of a structure some new development can be perceived.
The dynamics of being three partners has influenced every detail of the workshop. The teachers, for instance, can no longer take care of feedback and make plans along the day in the same informal .way as before. The team of teachers now have to arrange formal meetings in order to get everybody together. This meetings we think have been like a dynamo for the workshop. A creative setting where ideas on how to meet feedback, and how to arrange new sessions, easily have been found. Concerning the goal and our wish to increase group work activities we can verify that the fourth workshop was a success in this respect. Having students from three different countries represented in most of the sessions provided more variation in opinions and perspectives. It also has resulted in an even more open atmosphere between. students and teachers.

Conclusions

The conclusion of the experiences from these four courses is that we have to accept the fact that there a r e differences in the way of looking at pedagogy, democracy, culture, attitudes to alcohol and drugs, learning processes and the roles of the teachers not least. It shows that we still have a lot to learn from each other, but also that we have come far in optimising this experiment for didactics in higher education. Conflicts and contradictions are there to be solved, and there is absolutely no doubt

about the usefulness and fruitfulness in intensive courses like these.
In the spirit of European partnership, we suggest that we continue to develop our agenda in order to create a framework that is even more clear about academic and non-academic objectives. We have come far in setting academic goals. Our challenge must be to go on accommodating our diverse needs and cultural traditions in order to maximise the outcome of this unique exchange programme.'
We are looking forward to many years of productive co-operation in :the name of bringing down Cultural and learning barriers within the European context.

Evaluation of the Trinational Workshop 1993 (Germany, Sweden, The Netherlands)

Anne Killmann / Ute Knorrek

Introduction

The following article is an evaluation of the Trinational Workshop 1993 in Sweden out of the perspective of the german students. We (the editors) collected and structured contributions of the german students in order to give a chronological documentation and evaluation of our impressions of that Workshop. In the Epilogue we added our (the editors) impression of Workshop 1994 in the Netherlands.

These Workshops are meant to be intensive courses thus only a limited number of participants can join the Workshop (eight students and two lecturers of each country). This setting allows a real intensive working atmosphere as well as a good base for getting acquainted with one another.

I. Evaluation concerning the content of the Workshop 1993

1. Expectations / Apprehensions

We expected to get some information about Dutch and Swedish social work which we wanted to compare with German social work in order to search for differences and common grounds. This comparison should give us a clearer view for the German social work and for what is better/worse in the respective countries. We hoped to exchange methods and ideas by being in contact with Dutch and Swedish students. And of course we were happy to visit Sweden.

Apprehensions were that there might be a lack of exchange and communication in the way that each country presents the respective social work in an idealistic way by only showing the advantages in a competitive way. Another apprehension was to fear that one's English might not be sufficient for communication on an abstract level.

2. The Course of the Workshop

We started with a presentation of social work education and family legislation of the respective countries. Then we went into national groups and formulated questions about family arrangements to the other national groups which were again answered in national groups and presented to the plenum. That was a good tool for making a comparison and realizing differences.

The next step was the case study. All groups got the same case. The case had to be solved in national groups. Later on we presented the case study in small international groups and discussed about different and common approaches.

The last step of our theoretical course was the lecturers forum. The Swedish lecturer Ola Eriksson gave a lecture about the problem that the target person of the socialworker is rather seldom the „commission giver" of the socialworker and the domaine of social work. The German lecturer Gerd Gehrmann presented an ecological method called Environment Activating Method (EAM). The last day we made a trip to Stockholm where we visited some institutions and the University. We finished the Workshop with a short evaluation.

3. Outcome

(a) in general

It was a good exchange of ideas of social work. We became more openminded and put our ideas of social work in relation to the new ideas. The picture of social work in Germany became clearer by reflecting upon things we took for granted in our own system. It somehow was like a recharge of a battery by getting new ideas which supported former convictions about professional social work.

We realized the problem of where the borders of social work are (non voluntary intervention). Our impression was that professionalization tendencies seem to be quite similar in all the three countries such as the tendency away from therapy to putting the spot on the person in his/her environment (socio-ecological approach). Also the reputation of social work is placed despite of gradual differences in all the three countries at the lowest level of the academic hierarchy.

It was nice to become acquainted with one another we had a lot of fun. All in all it was a good start of our cooperation which should be intensified.

(b) What did we learn about German social work?

We expanded the knowledge of the German family legislation. Realizing the role of social work within the legal and societal frame we became more aware of the conflict how to avoid the perpetuation of discrimination named in this frame by finding emancipating ways of social work action.

The formulating of questions concerning family arrangements was very friutful for our group as we became aware of the above mentioned conflict of perpetuation of discrimination and emancipation within the German system. It was interesting that neither the Dutch nor the Swedish group understood the questions the way they were meant to be understood. Our assumption was that our questions were developed before the background of the German system. Although we did not get the desired answers we became conscious of things we took unconciously for granted before by realizing that these things are different handled in other countries.

Another important outcome concerns the case study. It was quite a hard work within the German group to find a compromise how to approach the case in general which then allowed a cooperation (preparation of cooperation by communication).

(c) What did we learn about Dutch social work?

We got some knowledge about the Dutch system, about social work education, about carried out methods in the practice of social work like Case Management and Hometraining. Dutch social work seems to have a rather environmental approach. The approach of multiloyality was very interesting for us, i.e. to work for different parties at the same time and how to handle this.

(d) What did we learn about Swedish social work?

We also got some knowledge about the Swedish system. By visiting institutions we got a good picture of the social work practice. During the Workshop we aquired information about social work education, Homebuilding which is called Families First Program, about the family law and we heard the very interesting lecture of Ola Eriksson about the „commission-giver“.

One remark: It became obviously that the first effect of comparative studies is that one learns more about the own system. The next step is then to become more acquainted with the other systems.

(e) criticism (positive/negative)

It was a good balance of groupwork, plenum and lecture. Although there sometimes was a lack of time to present the groupwork results in the plenum and to less space for students interests. The program was too fixed and not flexible enough - as it was too overloaded - for spontaneous arising needs. Sometimes the Workshop was too lecturer-oriented.

II. Perspectives and expectations for 1994

1. What do we still miss, what would we be interested in?

— Comparative statistical material

— A „realistoic assessment“ of the respective social work (because the national groups are not always representative for the respective social work)

— To get to know more applied methods

— When we worked in international groups there always seemed to be an agreement, there were rather no differences. Our question is whether there were misunderstandings which we did not realize. Maybe that could be proved by doing a case study in international teams or by adapting methods to the respective national (legal) conditions.

— What would be necessary to learn for us, if we would like to work in the Netherlands or Sweden (legal frame, history of social work and its traditions,..)?

— Working out the characteristics of professionality e.g. by case study.

— How is the assessment carried out in the Netherlands and Sweden according to generally accepted criteria?

— How is the following conflict integrated in the study course? (We call it structural conflict.) All three parts are interested in each other, but the different interests are never compatible with oneanother.

— Do you develop strategies how to deal with this unsolvable conflict?

— Do the methods take that conflict into account or do they just include the dealings with the client?

— Are there aims to strengthen the profession of social work? What about being organized into a union/professional association?

— Informations about Family Legislation in the Netherlands.

— How does Dutch social work work environmentally? (examples out of practice which demonstrates how to work concertely on/with the environment)

III. Exchange and cooperation

1. Which chances and opportunities could develop out of this?
Such cooperations widen one's horizon, away from regional or national to an european thinking about social work. Perspectives out of this could be:
– to work in international teams when we finish our studies
– we could organize a socialworker colloquium in a few years, so that we could stay in contact and still stimulate us
Also the exchange of methods is an important fact to open one's mind towards new ideas and to develop social work in the respective country.

IV. Epilogue

To sum up one can say that Workshop 1993 was very successful. We took many ideas home with us. Our impression is that it was a good start of cooperation. Therefore we were looking forward to intensifying our cooperation 1994 in the Netherlands and hoped that this will not be the last step of our cooperation.
Just arrived back in Frankfurt from Workshop 1994 in the Netherlands we would like to document our very fresh impressions of that Workshop.
This Workshop was our third Workshop and we realized that our interest raised from more detailed questions in the former Workshops to more general questions about social work approaches in this Workshop.
Although we experienced a development in these three Workshops one thing remained the same: One Workshop costs you the energy of three weeks (input) but you get new ideas and impulses for at least one year (output). So this form of courses is a very effective input-output relation. In this context we would like to thank all the lecturers for their efforts to organize such excellent courses. We experienced the Workshops as the *Highlights* of our nearly finished study course! It was an important way of widening one' horizon.